GETTING PAST "THE PIMP"

Management in the Sex Industry

Edited by Chris Bruckert and Colette Parent

The issue of third parties in the sex industry – individuals who are neither the client nor the service provider – has become especially urgent in our current socio-political context. Surprisingly, in spite of an emergence of critical scholarship on the sex industry, as well as recommendations by key governmental committees, little attention has been extended to examining the role of individuals labelled pimps, procurers, and traffickers.

Addressing the function of third parties on the street and indoors, *Getting Past "the Pimp"* incorporates solid empirical evidence including documentary analysis, 75 interviews with third parties, and 52 interviews with sex workers to unpack the roles and relationships of third parties in three sectors of the sex industry: incall/outcall, stripping, and street-based prostitution. Contrary to prevailing stereotypes that portray third parties as inherently abusive and controlling, these workers fulfil important roles and provide vital services as associates, fee-for-service hires, and agency owners or managers responsible for scheduling and arranging transportation and security. Much like a mainstream business, the sex industry rarely depends exclusively on client and worker to operate efficiently and safely. Collectively the essays in this volume make a compelling case for rethinking Canada's response to sex work, highlighting the limits of criminal justice "solutions" by drawing our attention to the experiences and perspectives of those whom they target.

CHRIS BRUCKERT is a professor in the Department of Criminology at the University of Ottawa.

COLETTE PARENT is a professor in the Department of Criminology at the University of Ottawa.

Getting Past "the Pimp"

Management in the Sex Industry

EDITED BY CHRIS BRUCKERT
AND COLETTE PARENT

UNIVERSITY OF TORONTO PRESS
Toronto Buffalo London

© University of Toronto Press 2018
Toronto Buffalo London
www.utorontopress.com

ISBN 978-1-4875-0320-8 (cloth)   ISBN 978-1-4875-2249-0 (paper)

Library and Archives Canada Cataloguing in Publication

Getting past "the pimp" : management in the sex
industry / edited by Chris Bruckert and Colette Parent.

Includes bibliographical references and index.
ISBN 978-1-4875-0320-8 (hardcover).   ISBN 978-1-4875-2249-0 (softcover)

1. Pimps.   2. Prostitution.   3. Sex-oriented businesses.
I. Bruckert, Chris, 1960–, editor II. Parent, Colette, 1947–, editor

HQ118.G48 2018   331.7′6130674   C2017-906125-9

This book has been published with the help of a grant from the Federation
for the Humanities and Social Sciences, through the Awards to Scholarly
Publications Program, using funds provided by the Social Sciences and
Humanities Research Council of Canada.

University of Toronto Press acknowledges the financial assistance to its
publishing program of the Canada Council for the Arts and the Ontario
Arts Council, an agency of the Government of Ontario.

Canada Council   Conseil des Arts
for the Arts   du Canada

Funded by the   Financé par le
Government   gouvernement
of Canada   du Canada

Canadä

ONTARIO ARTS COUNCIL
CONSEIL DES ARTS DE L'ONTARIO
an Ontario government agency
un organisme du gouvernement de l'Ontario

*This book is dedicated to
John Lowman and Francis Shaver.
With your pioneering sex work research, unwavering commitment
to social justice, and remarkable tenacity, you paved the way for
generations of scholars.*

Contents

Foreword

JENN CLAMEN

It is easy to hate the boss. The manager. The supervisor. People revel in it. The disdain is deeply engrained in our culture. Employees gather around water coolers to complain about their employers. The caricature of the cold-blooded, ruthless boss is reproduced in popular media and film, which both demonize and celebrate the elusive "man in charge." Now, factor in what is likely the most uncomfortable, taboo, and deeply challenging means of revenue production – prostitution. Exploitation in prostitution is generally assumed by the majority of the public – despite the fact that exploitation is not a required element of the criminal infractions related to third parties. Social framings of third parties, however, assume exploitation and promote enforcement of laws that, together, shape understandings of third parties in the sex industry as inherently exploitative and harmful.

In a less caricaturized version of the water-cooler scenario, a group of workers are complaining about work. The subject of conversation is their boss, but the subtext is their working conditions: expectations, hours, having to take on tasks not initially negotiated, lack of office supplies, sexual harassment, and verbal abuse. Capitalism creates conflicting interests between owners and managers of the means of production (who seek to maximize profit) and workers (who desire better and fairer working conditions). The culture of complaining about management and work in general is rooted in a history of fighting for workers' rights and better labour conditions.

When we view the nature of the relationships in sex work as exploitative, the commonalities with other labour sites are obscured. Since at least the 1970s, sex workers have argued that third party worker relationships in sex work are not inherently exploitative, but that criminalization creates antagonism between police and third parties, third parties and sex workers, and police and sex workers, leaving little recourse for sex workers facing increased exploitation. This was my point of entry when I began my advocacy work with people working in the sex industry. In 2001 I joined a group of sex workers in the United Kingdom who were attempting to unionize with one of the biggest trade unions; their work was focused on labour relations for sex workers. In 2003 in Canada, Kara Gillies and I founded the Canadian Guild for Erotic Labour, an entity that allowed us to engage with unions and discuss precarious working conditions, including those experienced by migrant sex workers. We originally intended to work with sex workers to negotiate with third parties to improve working conditions, but the criminalization of third parties meant not only that we could not engage with them for fear our advocacy would be deemed illegal, but that it was exceptionally difficult for sex workers to negotiate with third parties to improve working conditions. In short, the criminalization of third parties has far-reaching consequences for the conditions in which sex workers labour.

The barriers that criminalization poses to the improvement of working conditions is one of the reasons sex workers demand full decriminalization of the industry – which includes but is not limited to the removal of laws that criminalize clients, sex workers, and the people they work with – and access to occupational health and safety frameworks and employment standards.

Sex Workers' Rights Lobby or a "Pimp Lobby"?

One of the ways in which sex workers' fight to improve working conditions is undermined is through reference to, and promotion of, racialized and stereotypical language and fear-laden tropes about the sex industry, typically by people who want to abolish it. One of those tropes is the "pimp" – understood, as we see in this book, to be a racialized and unruly male. Not only does this language undermine third party work and the support systems utilized by those who perform such labour (and who may also employ "pimp language" within their own subculture) but it also uses and re-appropriates a discourse that is often used to insinuate violence; makes the use of "pimp language" a racist tool; and implies that the sex industry, and relationships within it, are inherently harmful.

With this disdain in mind, the movement for sex workers' rights and decriminalization is often falsely accused of being a "pimp lobby" – a movement that "promotes prostitution" in the "interests of pimps and profiteers." Sex workers, and indeed anyone who speaks to the rights to which workers in the sex industry should be entitled, are accused of being marionettes that parrot the words and interests of third parties. Because the language of "pimping" has historically been used as a racist tool by non-Black communities, framing the sex workers' rights movement as a "pimp lobby" reproduces stereotypes of sex work as inherently dangerous and exploitative, sex workers as incompetent and lacking agency, and sex workers' family, friends, and colleagues as immoral and untrustworthy. It discounts the reality that sex workers decide to work in the industry and overshadows the real issue: that in a criminalized context, sex workers are not necessarily able to negotiate the conditions under which they work. Employing the language of the "pimp lobby" is also a silencing technique that is effective precisely because of deep-seated mistrust of bosses in general, and bosses in the sex industry in particular – the idea, in other words, that having a boss is a "bad thing." Most importantly, it erases what actual exploitation in the sex industry actually looks like and blinds us to unfair labour practices. It says a great deal about the "pimp" trope's power that the word is used to try to discredit an entire global movement of workers advocating for their own rights.

None of this negates the fact that "pimp language" is, in fact, used by sex workers and some third parties alike – sometimes affectionately, and sometimes to indicate violence. "Pimps" do exist in the sex industry – although in a contemporary context, they exist more in the form of personal relationships than they do in the form of labour relationships. Some sex workers have "pimps." Most – as this and other research demonstrates – do not. Some are boyfriends, lovers, and people who facilitate sex work by seeking out clients. A "pimp" can be someone a sex worker loves and equally someone who is violent. Because sex workers' personal relationships are so often considered differently than the relationships of people outside the field of sex work, the violence that sex workers may experience is considered qualitatively different than the violence experienced by women in other contexts. Disturbingly, violence committed by "pimps" against sex workers is often ignored unless the sex worker not only denounces her "pimp" but also denounces her means of income.

Aside from trying to lay bare the realities and relationships that sex workers have with clients and third parties, part of the sex workers' rights movement also strives to revise historically stereotypical and damaging language: "sex work" and "third parties" are some of the fruits of that labour. These terms are not euphemisms. Rather, they reflect the focus on labour activity and allow a discussion about the harmful conditions that can exist in the production of labour – particularly labour that is at once on the margins, informal, gendered, and above all, criminalized.

The Struggle for Better Working Conditions

The movement for decriminalization and for sex workers' rights is grounded in human and labour rights, improving working conditions, and creating safe and healthy spaces for sex workers. In order to do that, we need to understand the role of third parties so that sex workers can improve their working relationships and address exploitative working conditions. It is a movement that endeavours to remove harmful legislation that criminalizes sex workers, clients, and third parties and that maintains the industry in an antagonistic relationship with otherwise mainstream protective mechanisms, including labour laws, law enforcement, and occupational health and safety.

Sex workers bear the brunt of the criminalization of third parties. In fact, it is sex workers who bear the brunt of criminalization in general. When we recognize that criminalization's harmful impacts move beyond arrest and into surveillance, unlawful eviction, abusive search and seizure, detention, interrogation, deportation, racial and social profiling, stigma, discrimination, and targeted violence, we can better understand the global impacts of criminalization and also recognize that it is impossible to criminalize one part of the industry without harming sex workers themselves.

The struggle for the removal of laws that criminalize third parties, clients, and sex workers is one that also seeks recognition for sex workers' right to better working conditions – including access to the same labour protections as workers in non-criminalized industries. It is also a struggle to distinguish labour exploitation from violence. Prohibitionists strategically fail to distinguish between labour exploitation, sexual exploitation, and sex work itself, at the same time as they use the language of the "pimp lobby" to maliciously "invisibilize" sex workers' struggle for recognition of their work and access to better working conditions.

The realities and functions of third parties in the sex industry are not approached or understood through a rights discourse by the majority of the public. Where people may have sympathy for sex workers' plight, they often fail to do the same for third parties. Understanding third parties as an essential part of sex work is increasingly being accepted, most recently by the highest court in Canada in *Canada (Attorney General) v. Bedford*. But this is often only true when the necessity for third parties is couched in a discourse of safety. Preferring to work with third parties for other reasons is a less vocalized reality, lest sex workers be accused of fighting for the rights of "those who profit." What about sex workers who cannot afford to run their own business or work for themselves? What about those who simply do not have the time or organizational capacity to seek out their own clients? What about people who prefer to work with others or benefit from working in groups? What about the working conditions of *all* people who work in the sex industry, including third parties? Acceptance of third parties in sex work tends to be quite classist, in this sense, as it assumes that entrepreneurship is the only way to avoid some kind of unavoidable exploitation. In reality, and as this research project demonstrated, many sex workers like to work with third parties and many sex workers are themselves simultaneously third parties; the roles in the industry overlap quite significantly. Many work as receptionists, drivers, or security while also selling sexual services. After many years of selling sex, some also move into management or ownership roles. There does not need to be anything inherently wrong with being or working for a boss, and sex workers should simultaneously be able to fight for better working conditions and the right to work with third parties for the utility of it.

We also need to start seeing the commonalities in labour exploitation across labour sites, and attribute labour rights to *all* workers, including sex workers. Sex workers encounter challenges when discussing labour exploitation in the sex industry because labour exploitation in sex work is so often treated as synonymous with sexual exploitation and sexual assault. This is true even in situations where sex workers are not contesting sex work itself but rather the conditions of their work. This does not mean that sex workers do not experience sexual assault. The challenge is that every instance of labour exploitation is assumed to be sexual assault, which overshadows the actual exploitation sex workers are trying to address. There is labour exploitation in the sex industry, and sexual assault in the lives of sex workers and other working folks. Sex workers need to be able to mitigate exploitation in the industry without the imposition of a sexual-exploitation framework.

Research in Community

The Rethinking Management in the Adult and Sex Industry research (henceforth Management Project) sought to reveal and analyse the roles of third parties and their relationships to sex workers. This framing focuses our attention on what people do, how they do it, and the ways power circulates in and through these relationships. The result is a much more nuanced portrait than the "pimp" trope would have us believe. In addition to the plethora of tasks that third parties engage in, and the nuanced levels of power that they have and share with sex workers, the research also uncovered how the onus of criminalization is shifted in a context where third parties are criminalized. This has the real, albeit presumably unintended, consequence of placing sex workers at risk.

Academic research is imbued with hierarchy and power. As such, it can marginalize the subjects of research and fail to recognize that participants are knowledge producers (and not, as is so often the framing, solely knowledge consumers or knowledge users). Traditional conventional research methods are a messy fit for stigmatized groups like sex workers. Such scholarship often isolates the community it is studying and imposes a framework that does not accurately represent, or do justice to, participants' nuanced realities. This strategy may be seen as a way to demonstrate "objectivity," and for researchers to avoid the mark of discredit ascribed to those who are sex workers and, by extension, to those who study them. Accordingly, researchers evoke the language of community rather than strive for the meaningful participation of community in knowledge production. In the same way that the term "pimp lobby" is used to discredit the sex workers' rights movement, sex work research is often discredited, and knowledge produced by people in the sex industry is often discounted. It is therefore even more important that research that engages community adheres to the highest ethical standard.

The Management Project attempted to create a new model of research that draws directly on sex workers' knowledge to centre the roles and relationships of third parties. While not falling within the textbook definition of community-based research, the Management Project illustrates the way research methods can be deployed to ensure ethical research and ethical management. This research straddles the boundaries of community research: while it is not community-based, it is, indeed, research for social change.

Employing the *philosophy* of community-based research, the Management Project responds to a direct need for community involvement in both research and in policy recommendations for the sex industry, and it employs rigorous research protocols to create a line of inquiry that is useful for sex workers, and that responds directly to what people working in the sex industry need to improve health and safety in the context of criminalization. From its conceptualization, the creation of the interview guide, interviews, the recruitment process, data analysis, and documentation, all fulfil the project's obligation to both the academy and to the community. To do this, we created an advisory committee of representatives from four Canadian sex worker organizations across the Maritimes, Québec, and Ontario: Stepping Stone (Halifax), Stella, l'amie de Maimie (Montreal), POWER (Ottawa), and Maggie's: Toronto Sex Workers Action Project (Toronto); some of these representatives, along with other community members, were trained to conduct interviews with third parties. The advisory committee also helped design and diffuse the research report and create a community tool that provided thought-provoking questions to consider when working with third parties. I coordinated the project and was responsible for community engagement.

"Who Knew?" The Third Party Work of Research Management

Designing research that is community-based in both ideology and practice is no easy feat, particularly for research around sex work, which is so often "othered" and marginalized in both research and broader social spaces. The Management Project created, unintentionally and perhaps ironically, an ethical model of management that places the worker at the centre – an approach that, in the legitimate and privileged context of the academy, could serve as a model. We designed a project that centred ethics and community empowerment – two cornerstones of community-based research. In fact, so much of the way the research was organized mirrored the relationships and roles within the sex industry. This helped us reflect on third party relationships with sex workers in a way that is so often out of reach because of the stigma surrounding the relationship between a sex worker and a third party. Of course, creating a model for ethical research and management proved to be easier in a context where criminalization does not impede communication, negotiation, and support between researchers, interviewers, interviewees, transcribers, and the other workers employed.

The negotiation of power in this research very closely paralleled the negotiation of power we observed in third party worker relationships.

The researchers, similar to owners or bosses, determined the overall direction of the research, the project coordinator (manager) coordinated between interviewers (sex workers) and interviewees (clients), and also organized a schedule of interviews based on the interviewers' availabilities. Interviewers were "on call," as many are within the sex industry, subject to the availability of the client (interviewee). This kind of flexibility and support is also vital in any informal labour market – including in the sex industry.

Re-envisioning Third Parties

It is only by understanding the work of third parties from a labour perspective that we can seek to improve conditions for sex workers. If the labour relationship in itself is viewed as dangerous and exploitative there is no chance to identify where labour conditions need improving. That "icky" look that people get on their face when they think of third parties in the sex industry is often an indication of the biased view that selling sex is particularly degrading and inferior to other work and that third parties in the industry are distinct from other management in a capitalist context. For sex workers and third parties this is often not the case. This book allows us to look at sex work and the people that sex workers work for and with – or whom they hire – without the cloud of stigma. Further, it pushes us to think about how that stigma can itself cause harm to sex workers. It invites us to look at the people dismissed as "pimps" from a labour perspective rather than one of assumed exploitation.

Jenn Clamen
Management Project coordinator and activist
for the rights of sex workers

Acknowledgments

First and foremost, we would like to thank the sex workers and third parties who trusted us with their stories and took the time to speak with us: without them there would have been no book to write.

This project would never have come to fruition without the members of the research team: Jenn Clamen, Patrice Corriveau, Leslie Jeffrey, Tuulia Law, and Maria Nengeh Mensah – all of whom have contributed to this collection. We are also grateful to the many people who shared their expertise and wisdom and contributed to the research project in various ways: Sarah Beer, Leila Beheshti, Frédérique Chabot, Cynthia Dubé, Elya Durisin, Mickael Chacha Enriquez, Lyne Généreux, Kara Gillies, Julie Marceau, Sébastien Lachambre, Le-ann Patton, Kelly Phipps, Pascale Robitaille, and Tara Santini.

We are immensely grateful to the staff and volunteers at the sex worker rights organizations that collaborated in the project – their insight, support, and assistance were invaluable. In particular we would like to acknowledge the contributions of Émilie Laliberté, representing Stella; Rene Ross, representing Stepping Stone; Keisha Scott, representing Maggie's; and Emily Symons, representing POWER.

We thank the anonymous reviewers for their careful and thoughtful comments; the manuscript is improved because of the helpful feedback you provided.

To the staff at the University of Toronto Press, we express our heartfelt gratitude; particular thanks go to Douglas Hildebrand for his enthusiastic guidance throughout the publishing process.

Finally, we would like to thank the Social Sciences and Humanities Research Council of Canada for its financial contributions to the Management Project, without which this research would not have been possible.

GETTING PAST "THE PIMP"

Management in the Sex Industry

Introduction: Revisioning
Third Parties in the Sex Industry

CHRIS BRUCKERT

Pimps, procurers, and *traffickers* – the words evoke powerful emotions. Indeed it is hard to avoid the pervasive narrative embedded in the collective imagination and reproduced in popular culture, in the media, and in the proclamations of politicians. The "pimp"[1] is in many ways a classic folk devil: mere mention conjures up images of a racialized man who exploits a "stable" of young women he has lured or tricked into prostitution and whom he controls through violence, manipulation, and/or drugs. As such it is impossible to ignore that this "common knowledge" draws heavily on racist and classist tropes and reflects deep-seated fears of Black men (O'Connell, 1998; Davis, 1983; Jeffrey and MacDonald, 2006; see also Mensah, this collection).[2]

Over the last two decades a discourse that first emerged in the Progressive Era's fear of the "white slave trade" has re-emerged (Toupin, 2013) and the "pimp" narrative has become increasingly entwined with another, perhaps even more egregious, folk devil: the trafficker. Here we see the influence of neo-prohibitionist feminists for whom sex work reflects and reinforces gender inequity and is, at its core, violence against women: an institution that, regardless of sector, strategies, or legal regime, is inherently violent –"a form of sexualized male violence" (Day, 2008, 28) that exists "at the intersection of incest, rape, battery, and torture" (Holsopple, 1999, 49) and "destroys not only the integrity of the body, but also the integrity of the identity itself" (Comte, 2014, 200). Women's participation in the industry is neatly (if tautologically) explained by framing sex workers as vulnerable victims susceptible to being abused, manipulated, and/or coerced by men.[3] From this point of departure "any man or woman who induces, promotes, and profits from the prostitution of women and children" (Holsopple, 1999, 47) is an exploiter.[4] If prostitution is sexual exploitation it is also trafficking. In either case "the prostitute's consent is irrelevant, because you can never consent to sexual exploitation" (Ratansi, 2007, 5). It follows that, according to neo-prohibitionist feminists, "prostitution is [not] qualitatively different from trafficking" (Farley et al., 2004, 33) and the terms *pimp* and *trafficker* have become fused into a new category of "pimps/traffickers."[5] Conceptually speaking, the threat posed by those who work for, with, or hire sex workers has expanded; while the "pimp" is largely discursively affiliated with the street sector, traffickers are understood as operating both on the street and in the indoor sex industry.

The narrative has expanded in another way as well, resulting in a compelling, if rather incongruent, morality tale. At the same time as sex workers are framed as "other," "pimps/traffickers" are presented as so pervasive and so insidious that "anyone's daughter" is at risk of falling prey. This narrative was front and centre in the media coverage (2012–15) of the infamous Ottawa "teen pimp ring" involving three young women who used a range of tactics including blackmail, violence, and drugs to compel other underage women to provide sexual services.[6] For the most part the reporting – filled with salacious details, titillating "facts," a great deal of hyperbole, and much condemnation of the sex industry – offers a case study of trauma porn. For example, one of the accused, described as "manipulative" and a victim of her environment, was chastised because she "gravitated toward others in the sex trade while in custody" (Seymour, 2015). Above all it became a "stunning cautionary tale about the perils of social media" (OPS Staff Sgt. John McGetrick quoted in Renni, 2012) giving rise to regulatory-protectionist rhetoric warning of the predatory potential lurking behind every (social media) post. In the face of this omnipresent threat readers were chastised for failing to recognize that "this could happen to their daughter, their niece, or their neighbour's kid" (Trihn, 2012), and were urged to diligently surveil their daughters (Renni, 2012). In other words, a story that could have given rise to a nuanced national debate – after all, the perpetrators shared few of the stereotypical characteristics of "pimps," although the repeated references (and images of) community housing projects ensured readers understood the accused's (under)class status – was instead used to, once again, justify greater regulation of young women.[7] But there was another conceptual sleight of hand at play; presenting the story as "unusual" or "shocking" reinforced the normative framing of exploitative men in organized crime networks – aspects that were absent from the actual case but which are at the heart of conservative and neo-prohibitionist feminist claims.

Indeed the neo-prohibitionist framing has become pervasive. We see it in policing initiatives that, ostensibly in the interests of "saving victims," alienate, intimidate, and further marginalize sex workers;[8] we see it in media accounts that seamlessly fuse trafficking, "pimping," and commercial sex;[9] and we see it in the law. At the time the research that informs this collection was being conducted, third parties were criminalized under *Criminal Code* sections 210(1) (being an owner-operator of a bawdy house) and 212(1) (procuring and living on the avails of another's prostitution). The 2013 Supreme Court of Canada decision in *Bedford*[10] upheld a lower-court ruling that two of the laws criminalizing third parties – specifically the bawdy house (CC s. 210) and living on the avails (CC s. 212(1) (j)) provisions – inhibited sex workers' ability to access the services of third parties that decrease their vulnerability to violence and therefore contravened section 7 of the *Canadian Charter of Rights and Freedoms*.[11] In response, the Conservative government of the day introduced the *Protection of Communities and Exploited Persons Act*. While the bill was roundly condemned by sex workers, it was widely endorsed by the religious right, social conservatives, and – in a rather striking example of "carceral feminism" (Bernstein 2007a)[12] – neo-prohibitionist feminists. At the hearings harsh laws against "pimps" – understood to be "shrewd businessmen" (Miller, 2014) who "spin a web of lies around their victims ... [until] the psychological trap is complete and inescapable" (Truong, 2014) – were supported. Keira Smith-Tague (2014) of Vancouver Rape Relief, negating the evidence and the testimony of sex workers who problematized the criminalized context in which they are obliged to work, asserted that "the source of the harm in prostitution is from the men who buy them and sell them." So powerful is the "pimp" trope, and so accessible the subtext, that those who endeavoured to complicate the conversation by, for example, drawing attention to the empirical[13] and experiential evidence that third parties provide services (e.g., security, workplace locations, business and administrative support) that sex workers desire were, as Jenn Clamen notes in the foreword to this collection, vilified as part of a "pimp lobby," or in the words of feminist lawyer Gunilla Ekberg (2014), "pro-violation constituencies."

The law, which came into effect on 6 December 2014, revised and updated the procuring laws (CC s. 286.3) and also added a number of additional sections that replicate the provisions overturned by the Supreme Court of Canada vis-à-vis third parties. Under the current legal regime third parties are prohibited from materially benefitting from the sexual services of another (CC s. 286.2). Importantly, the law codifies established case law by specifying that those in "legitimate living arrangements" or those with "legal or moral obligations" are exempted, but it criminalizes all third parties operating in the context of a "commercial enterprise." In addition, "everyone who knowingly advertises an offer to provide sexual services for consideration" can now be criminally charged under section 286.4 of the *Criminal Code*. Third parties are also increasingly being charged with trafficking offences.[14] Surprisingly, given that the United Nations Palermo Protocol[15] specifically refers to trafficking as the movement of people by organized syndicates, in Canada most charges under the 2005 law involve neither criminal networks nor the movement of victims but, rather, are layered over prostitution charges (Millar and O'Doherty, 2015). This further affirms that in Canada there is a "fragile distinction between trafficking and procurement" (Roots, 2013, 32). In short, the *activities of all third parties in commercial sexual enterprises are criminalized*. This means that agents, brothel owners, drivers, security, and advertisers – regardless of the services they provide or their relationship to sex workers – are vulnerable to being criminally convicted and labelled "pimps," "procurers," and/or "traffickers."

What does this socio-legal context mean for how sex workers are constituted in legal and "everyday" discourse? Embedded in the "pimp/trafficker" trope is a conceptualization of sex workers associated with, or working for, third parties as incompetent neo-liberal subjects incapable of making the "right" choices (Bruckert and Hannem, 2013). Evoking the same strategy long used to regulate women (Kilty, 2013), sex workers are medicalized and framed as deluded, incompetent victims who:

> Share certain background factors which make them more vulnerable to being lured into a life of prostitution. These pre-existing vulnerabilities include childhood physical and sexual abuse or emotional neglect, dissociation, isolation or alienation from family, lack of education and job skills and low self-esteem. (Attorney General of Canada, 2011)

Indeed sex workers are constituted as so incompetent that criminally charging (under CC s. 213 (1) (a), (b) and now under the newly crafted 213(1.1)) these individuals – whom the law explicitly defined as "victims" – was justified by then justice minister Peter MacKay (2014) as providing "police that initial discretion at the front end to encourage prostitutes [to exit]."

In short the very narrative that highlights victimization also affirms stigmatic assumptions about "the kind of woman who is a sex worker" – that is, someone who is damaged, socially isolated, suffering from low self-esteem, uneducated, a survivor of sexual abuse, intellectually disabled, mentally ill, and/or generally speaking so oppressed she is incapable of recognizing her own best interests. Of course negating sex workers' agency, competence, and abilities neatly justifies their silencing. The manipulative "pimp/trafficker" and the vulnerable sex worker form a conceptual dyad that draws heavily on deeply embedded gender, class, and racial stereotypes. This congruence with existing framing may in part explain why the script is so firmly embedded: it is an "intuitive" narrative that neatly replicates and affirms existing tropes without challenging our normative assumptions of the "other." As Mensah notes in this collection, "representations of the 'pimp' and 'pimping' make sense for us because they draw on lived experience and recognizable situations, and associate these with concepts and symbols that allow us to talk about them." They also function "as a blinder ... preventing access to knowledge about various other kinds of third party work in the sex industry" (30).

What happens when we shed these blinders and trouble these convenient, intuitive truths that infuse not only the media but also, as Corriveau and Parent (this collection) demonstrate, scholarly work as well? When we rethink "common sense" assumptions about sex workers and those with whom they work? When we refuse to participate in the discrediting and negation that is inherent in stigmatization? What happens when we recognize that the decision to sell sexual services, like all decisions, is inevitably constrained by social and structural factors but also respects the agency and competence of sex workers? When we embrace an epistemological position that recognizes individuals as the experts of their own lives? When we take seriously sex workers' assertion that sex work – whether done independently or in a managed context – is an income-generating activity? This is the point of departure for this book. It is a framing supported by a robust body of social science evidence[16] that moves beyond stereotypes and, rather than defining sex workers as victims and categorizing all individuals with whom they work for or with as "pimps/traffickers," offers a more nuanced position that recognizes that "not all victims of trafficking are prostitutes, nor are all prostitutes victims of trafficking" (Sanghera, 2005, 11).

It is for these reasons that we are careful in our use of the loaded language of "pimps," traffickers, and exploiters. It is also for these reasons that we attend to the multiplicity of *managerial* roles rather than focus solely on the ubiquitous manager. In the business world third parties are individuals or entities, other than the buyer and the seller (the principals), involved in an arrangement, contract, agreement, or transaction. They can be, for example, organizers, promoters, agents, middle-persons, service providers, and, of course, managers. Third parties often mediate the commercial services that increasingly permeate our lives. Examples would include agencies that arrange house cleaning or organize temporary (or more permanent) office, domestic, security, or agricultural staff; special event organizers who plan weddings or children's birthday parties; investment consultants hired to manage personal financial well-being; and realtors who sell houses. The list is long and varied. Not all service provision is mediated through a third party of course – contract or self-employed workers offer their services directly to clients or work in association with other third parties (e.g., an individual can hire a limousine driver to take their teen to the prom, but these chauffeurs may have arrangements with wedding planners). Moreover, as the service provision market has expanded into areas previously considered the private domain (Hochschild, 2003), the purchase of services and commercial third parties play an increasingly large role in our personal relations. Certainly, third parties are implicated in organizing the care of children or elderly parents – there are agencies that match caregivers with clients interested in purchasing this service as well as agencies that coordinate workers (often women from the Philippines) to come to Canada and provide child (or elder) care. In short, third parties are intertwined in the economic, social, and personal lives of Canadians and they operate at multiple, intersecting, and overlapping levels. In general, these third parties provide (more or less) valuable services that allow us, as consumers or workers, to access skills and competencies we do not possess, to avoid tasks we do not enjoy, to free up time for other activities, or to connect with individuals/businesses with whom we do not, in the normal course of our lives, have contact.

This collection demonstrates that sex industry third parties fulfil the same sorts of roles that third parties perform in mainstream businesses. Some are agency owners and/or managers who engage sex workers in an employee-like relationship, others are associates who work with sex workers, and some are hired by sex workers to provide services on a fee-for-service basis (see "Who are third parties?," this collection; Bruckert and Law, 2013). In fact there is almost always someone else involved in a commercial sexual transaction that is neither the client nor the worker – in other words, a third party. It may be someone who receives financial remuneration for the services they offer (e.g., providing transportation, web space); it may be a friend or partner who, as a favour, agrees to be the sex worker's "safe call"; it may be an experienced sex worker who teaches a novice (for a fee or percentage) about the industry and how to keep safe; or it may be an agency owner who schedules, books, provides security, and arranges transportation in exchange for a reasonable (or outrageous) percentage of the worker's fees.[17] It may, as Arlene Pitts (2015) has recently argued, be an informal arrangement between a sex worker and the individual who supplies her with illicit substances and also offers her a measure of security and protection. And while third parties are largely vilified, the alternative – sex workers labouring in isolation without support or services – should give us pause. Indeed it is hard to imagine how the absence of third parties would not exacerbate the vulnerability of sex workers – especially for the most marginal among them.

While some third parties offer sex workers valuable services in exchange for reasonable compensation others are, as the stereotype suggests, controlling, abusive, and violent individuals who economically and/or sexually exploit those with whom they work. Our intent is neither to deny the existence of these social actors nor to obscure or gloss over the very real problems they represent – it is the opposite. By shedding light on this hidden sector and the roles of third parties who provide managerial support in both formal and informal ways, we draw attention to the complexity and array of relationships sex workers have with third parties and recognize, as Corriveau and Parent write, that control can be "exerted on a continuum from draconian to democratic" (71).[18] This alerts us to the importance of recognizing that the violence and abuse sex workers experience may be entangled with, for example, an abusive interpersonal relationship. It also positions us to think about the role criminal law plays in inhibiting the development of industry standards and best practices at the same time as it alerts us to the negative repercussions when – as we see in strip clubs (Law, this collection) – administrative regulation is informed by stigmatic assumptions. Moreover, rather than reproducing simplistic (and spurious) overgeneralizations about third parties as inevitably exploitative, we can think about the impact the de facto lack of workplace protections has on the entrenchment of unfair labour practices (e.g., excessive rules, unfair hiring practices, expectations of unpaid work); an issue Bruckert and Law (Chapter 4) and Jeffrey (Chapter 6) highlight in this collection.

Finally, when we abandon stigmatic assumptions we recognize that there is an inevitable corollary to sex workers' assertion that "sex work is work."[19] If sex work is work, then those who hire, collaborate with, or provide assistance to sex workers are also working. That recognition positions us to draw on broader labour, work, and management literature to think about third parties in the sex industry as workers, bosses, supervisors, managers, and service providers; it also allows us to situate – as we do throughout this collection – sex industry labour policies and practices in the broader context of work in neo-liberal times. To this end we also draw attention to parallel processes and practices in mainstream employment. For example, as Jeffrey tells us in Chapter 6:

> The flexibility of work in the sex industry, while it is one of the sector's attractions, also opens up the possibility of exploitation of labour when owners/managers exert control over the labour process without treating employees as actual employees – resulting in "flexibilization" and precariousness rather than flexibility as is the case in so many other industries in this neo-liberal era. (132)

Methodological Notes

In this collection we draw on the findings from a large study funded by the Social Science and Humanities Research Council (SSHRC) that examined management in the Canadian sex industry (hereafter Management Project) to complicate the narrative about third parties. We have been dismissed as part of the "pimp lobby," criticized for listening to what third parties ("exploiters," "pimps," and "traffickers") have to say, and condemned for challenging "common sense" tropes with empirical evidence. As social scientists, the researchers in this project felt strongly that perpetuating a discourse by silencing individuals on the basis of stereotypical assumptions is unconscionable; indeed, it is precisely for this reason that it is important to speak with third parties and listen to what they say. Moreover, as feminists and critical scholars, our epistemological point of departure obliges us to respectfully attend to the experiential voice and centre experience (Morris and Bunjun, 2007; Kovach, 2005; Reinharz, 1993) recognizing "that even the most conscious social actors are not immune to the deeply embedded social constructs that condition our understanding of the world ... [and] when those with limited economic, social, and cultural capital attempt to challenge the discourses, they most often go unheard and unheeded" (Hannem and Bruckert, 2012, 176).

The Management Project was neither a community-based nor a participatory action research. Indeed it was led by a bilingual interdisciplinary academic team assembled with an eye to ensuring diverse theoretical lines of sight (Mensah is a cultural studies scholar; Jeffrey comes from political science; Corriveau has a background in law and justice; Parent and Law are criminologists; Bruckert is trained in sociology). The investigators, all of whom contributed to this collection, were, however, committed to ensuring the project was pertinent for sex workers who labour either for or with third parties or hire them.[20] Many of the researchers had established relationships with the sex work communities in their regions based on histories of careful and respectful engagement. We were therefore not only cognizant that sex worker rights organizations have unparalleled knowledge about the sex industry but were well positioned to collaborate in a meaningful, respectful, and ultimately exceptionally productive way with the community.[21] Four sex worker rights groups, operating in the geographic areas of this project (Maggie's, Toronto; POWER, Ottawa; Stella, Montreal; Stepping Stone, Halifax), were invited to participate. Their contribution proved invaluable: among other things they facilitated an "environmental scan" to ensure researchers had a holistic understanding of the issues, were sensitized to challenges, understood shifting dynamics, and grasped some of the nuances of "insider" language around third parties. Moreover, representatives sat on our Community Advisory Committee providing advice at various pivotal moments throughout the research process (e.g., feedback and input into framing the research questions, media analysis keywords, recruitment strategies, refining the interview guide).[22] We were fortunate to be able to hire as a research coordinator Jenn Clamen (who wrote the foreword for this collection), a long-time sex worker rights advocate who brought to the project important knowledge and prodigious skill.[23]

The Management Project first sought to understand the social, legal, and discursive context by undertaking a literature review and analysing media representations, legal/judicial decisions, and parliamentary reports. This contextual analysis informs all the chapters in this collection but is highlighted especially in Chapter 1, "The Representation of the 'Pimp,' " by Maria Nengeh Mensah. The heart of the project was the two phases of interviews. In order to provide the reader with an understanding of our methodological approach the research protocol is presented here while demographics of the entire sample are detailed in Chapter 2, "Who are Third Parties?"; specifics regarding the various subsamples (street, incall/outcall, and erotic dance) are presented in the applicable substantive chapters.

The first phase of interviews entailed a series of seventy-five in-depth, face-to-face interviews[24] (lasting between one and four hours) with individuals who work (or worked) as third parties in various sectors of the sex industry (street-based, incall/outcall, and strip clubs) in the Maritimes, Québec, and Ontario. A broad definition was employed: "an individual who does (or did since the year 2000) for (direct or indirect) financial compensation or benefit, supervise, control, facilitate, and/or coordinate the labour process (what s/he does, when and where) and/or the labour practices (how s/he works) of an adult sex worker." This expansive framing[25] reflected sex worker community knowledge that while managers clearly organize, supervise, facilitate, and coordinate the labour of sex workers, they are not the only players to take on these roles. Rather, there are a host of social actors who assume administrative tasks – receptionists, drivers, agents, location providers, security personnel, and sex workers; all of them are in fact third parties vulnerable to criminal charges on the basis of their professional activities. They may not self-identify as a manager in spite of the fact that their role is (or was) to supervise, control, facilitate, and/or coordinate the labour of sex worker(s): the very activities captured under the procuring law (Bruckert and Law, 2013). Such a framing had the additional benefit of ensuring we heard the perspectives and unique insights of individuals who are neither sex workers nor managers. This makes intuitive sense; for in the sex industry, as in any mainstream enterprise, an administrative assistant navigates day-to-day tensions and has a particular perspective on the working of a business while not being invested in preserving the corporate image in the same way his or her employer is likely to be.

Given the limited scholarship on third parties in the sex industry, a data-collection approach that produced rich and textured knowledge, positioned researchers to explore a range of areas, and provided participants with the opportunity to reflect on their experiences was called for. Accordingly, interviewers were trained in in-depth interviewing techniques and an interview guide was developed that employed non-directive, open-ended queries to elicit the stories and perceptions of participants. We also used semi-structured interventions to probe experiences, and some more structured questions to obtain information on policies and practices.

While the interviews with third parties were intended to be wide-ranging and exploratory, the interviews with sex workers who had laboured for, or with, a third party since the year 2000[26] were a mechanism to verify information, add nuance to our findings on third party policies and practices, and gain insight into how they "play out" for sex workers. Using sector-specific interview guides based on preliminary findings from the interviews with third parties, 10 focus-group interviews (lasting between two and three hours each) with 52 sex workers[27] who work or had worked for or with third parties, were conducted. All participants were women (including 3 who were trans) and while the ethnicity of all the women is not known, of the 39 who indicated ethnicity the overwhelming majority (27) were white, while 5 women identified as Indigenous and white, 3 as Black, 3 as Indigenous; and one as Black and Indigenous.

Focus groups are an approach that "explicitly use group interaction as part of the data-gathering method" (Berg, 2009, 158) and create a space where participants can explore and discuss issues, collectively refine their understandings, and reflect on unanticipated issues that emerge. The lively conversations and animated responses of focus-group members to some of our assertions, or the stories of other sex workers, provided invaluable insights into industry norms and worker expectations.

Recruiting research participants involved in criminalized behaviours poses obvious challenges[28] that are exacerbated when the population is not only stigmatized but also demonized (as is the case for third parties) or dismissed and negated a priori as victims (as is sometimes the case for sex workers who work for or with third parties). Our success at realizing a robust sample speaks to the trust relationships a number of the researchers have with the sex work community but also to the measures we implemented – for example, we attempted to minimize barriers to participation by, among other measures, providing a toll-free phone number and dedicated voice mail, responding promptly to queries, and offering an honorarium to cover expenses. We also endeavoured to minimize, to the extent possible, a particular methodological issue that sometimes plagues studies on the sex industry:

> Although random sampling of sex workers and customers is impossible, too often the findings and conclusions drawn from convenience and snowball samples are not properly qualified as nongeneralizable. Victimization studies are a case in point. Street prostitutes appear to experience high rates of violence in the course of their work, but the samples used in most studies consist of people who contacted service agencies, were approached on the street, or were interviewed in jail. (Weitzer, 2005, 938)

To realize as diverse a sample as possible the project used a wide range of recruitment strategies to ensure our sample extended well beyond researchers' networks and those of the sex worker rights organizations that advised us. Indeed, while we make no claim of a representative sample – nor could anyone in the current socio-legal context – the richness (and at times disparity) of the data suggests we were successful. Methods included: placing advertisements in newspapers; doing interviews with radio and print media; press releases; posting recruitment information on CERB-endorsed (Canadian Escort Review Board) sites and listings; sending emails or mailing recruitment flyers to incall and outcall establishments and strip clubs; distributing information on sex-work-related email listservs; distributing recruitment information through sex worker rights organizations and other organizations whose clientele include sex workers; distributing research information to (select) defence lawyers in Québec; circulating information among the various personal, social, and professional contacts of the researchers, Community Advisory Committee members, and interviewers; and snowball recruitment.

Individual and focus-group interviews were recorded and transcribed verbatim. Each phase of the research was coded separately and the anonymized transcripts team-coded using qualitative research software (NVivo®). A semi-organic codebook was developed that included conceptual codes informed by theory and the existing literature, information codes from the interview guide, and grounded codes that emerged from the interviews. Throughout this process, we paid particular attention to the relationships to, and needs of, sex workers. Once the coding of each interview set was completed, a "horizontal" trans-interview analysis (Pires, 1997) was undertaken to identify points of convergence and disjuncture, and analytic frameworks were developed that "made sense" of the findings within each phase. This analytic process proved fruitful and allowed for new and unanticipated findings to emerge from the data. For example, the typology of agencies, associates, and contractors is a grounded finding that emerged from the research. Ultimately, the multiple intersecting methods employed in this research allowed for the accumulation of distinctive data sets (documentary analysis, interviews, focus groups) on the same topic, generating multiple lines of sight in order to realize a more global understanding; in methodological terms we used triangulation (Denzin, 1978).

Outline of the Book

The rich, nuanced, and complex data that emerged from the documentary analysis and interviews, viewed through our diverse disciplinary lenses, informs the chapters in this book. The book starts with "The Representation of the 'Pimp': A Barrier to Understanding the Work of Third Parties in the Adult Canadian Sex Industry." In this chapter Maria Nengeh Mensah, writing as a cultural studies scholar, unpacks the notion of "common sense" before examining the representation of the "pimp" in popular culture and the media. Drawing on an original archive, she unpacks the conceptual worlds of the adult sex industry – location, gangsterism, violence, and human trafficking – in order to tease out the ways racial stereotypes, gender tropes, and stigmatic markings affirm otherness. It is precisely this question of "the other" that underpins Chapter 2: "Who are Third Parties? Pathways In and Out of Third Party Work," by Chris Bruckert. This chapter draws on the interviews with third parties to trouble the prevailing narrative. Highlighting the diverse roles of third parties (e.g., agents, mentors, worksite providers, peer facilitators, bouncers/security, DJs) and speaking to challenges, the chapter pivots on the question of pathways. It asks: why would individuals, in the face of such negative narratives about "the kind of people who are third parties," elect to do this work? And what, if anything, prompted them to move on to other employment?

The next three chapters examine management in different sectors of the commercial sex industry. We start with Patrice Corriveau and Colette Parent's chapter "Through the Voices of Female Sex Workers: The Street Manager," which juxtaposes the assertions from the literature to those of sex workers who work for street managers. Chapter 4, "The Business of Sex Businesses: Third Parties in the Incall/Outcall Sector," by Chris Bruckert and Tuulia Law, examines the commercial indoor sex industry and highlights the ways competing interests between third parties and sex workers play out in these criminalized spaces. The final sex industry sector examined is that of erotic dance (Chapter 5: "Third Parties and the Employment Relationship: The Erotic Dance Sector in Ontario"). Here Tuulia Law situates strip club labour practices in the broader socio-legal context before unpacking roles, responsibilities, and labour practices. Common themes run through these three chapters: the banality of management; the complexity of relationships between participants in the sex industry; how pervasive and entrenched stigmatic assumptions play out in delegitimization, as well as symbolic (interpersonal) and structural stigma;[29] and – perhaps inevitably, given the complexity of power relations – resistance (Foucault, 1978, 95). These chapters also highlight the negative impact of criminalization, an issue that is foregrounded in the final chapter, "Managing Sex Work: Bringing the Industry in from the Cold," which pulls together this collection's various threads. In this policy chapter Leslie Jeffrey brings stigma, discourse, and law together to highlight the distinction "between being managed as a problem and bad management as a problem." Collectively the book makes a compelling case for rethinking Canada's response to sex work, highlighting the limits of criminal justice "solutions" by drawing our attention to the experiences and perspectives of those whom they target. At the same time, the evidence presented in this book underlines the risk of implementing bureaucratic solutions that fail to centre the experiences and knowledge of current sex workers – precisely those individuals who are most impacted by regulation and who must be front and centre in any policy decisions.

Notes

1 To reflect our understanding that the term *pimp* is an ideologically loaded concept, the word (and its derivatives) are presented in either quotations or italics throughout this collection.

2 The experience of Mactar Mbaye, a twenty-three-year-old Montreal-area entrepreneur, illustrates the enduring racist tropes informing the "pimp" narrative. In February 2016 the Senegalese immigrant was shocked and embarrassed when he suddenly found himself – in the midst of conducting a job interview with a young woman he wished to hire – being questioned by police at a Laval Tim Horton's. The police were responding to a 911 call made by one of the patrons who had assumed he was a "pimp" recruiting a (white) sex worker (Chin, 2016).

3 For recent in-depth analysis of the feminist prohibitionist position see for example Levy and Jakobsson, 2013; Parent and Bruckert, 2013; and Chu and Glass, 2013.

4 See for example Raphael and Myers-Powell, 2010; Raphael et al., 2010, 2009; Day, 2008; Lakeman et al., 2004; Farley, 2003, 2004; Poulin, 2003; Holsopple, 1999; Barry, 1995; Louis, 1991; Hoigard and Finstad, 1992.

5 See also Raphael et al., 2010.

6 Ironically, given the demonization of clients, this came to the attention of the police when a would-be client made a report (Lofaro, 2014).

7 A link Mensah (this collection) makes by drawing on the work of Jeffrey and MacDonald, (2006) on the 1990s Halifax "pimping panic."

8 For example in January 2014, as part of Operation Northern Spotlight, the members of the Ottawa Police Service's anti-trafficking unit posed as clients in order to book appointments with independent sex workers. The women, expecting a client, were instead greeted by four male police officers on their doorstep. As the Ottawa-area sex workers rights group POWER points out, while "ostensibly to ensure that no coercion is taking place [these initiatives have] the impact of intimidating sex workers, violating their right to privacy and putting their confidentiality and safety at risk" (POWER, 2014).

9 See for example Davidson, 2016.

10 *Canada (Attorney General) v. Bedford*, 2013 SCC 72.

11 Section 7 of the *Canadian Charter of Rights and Freedoms* states that "Everyone has the right to life, liberty and security of the person and the right not to be deprived thereof except in accordance with the principles of fundamental justice." The courts also overturned *Criminal Code* section 213.1 (c), which prohibited communication for the purposes of prostitution in a public place, and 210, which criminalized not only keeping a bawdy house but also being an inmate or "found in."

12 Carceral feminism is a tendency of some feminists to embrace criminal justice solutions for social problems.

13 See for example Bruckert and Law, 2013; Gillies, 2013.

14 Defined in *Criminal Code* section 279.01 (01) as "anyone who recruits, transports, transfers, receives, holds, conceals or harbours a person, or exercises control, direction or influence over the movements of a person, for the purpose of exploiting them or facilitating their exploitation."

15 The United Nations "Protocol to prevent, suppress and punish trafficking in persons, especially women and children," adopted in 2000, came into effect on 25 December 2003.

16 See for example Bowen, Bungay, and Zangger, 2015; Benoit et al., 2014; van der Meulen, Durisin, and Love, 2013; Law, 2011; O'Doherty, 2011; Bruckert and Chabot, 2010; Brock, 2009; van der Meulen and Durisin, 2008; Parent and Bruckert, 2006, 2005; Jeffrey and MacDonald, 2006; Mensah, 2006; Ross, 2006; Lewis et al., 2005; Shaver, 2005, 1996, 1993; Bruckert, Parent, and Robitaille, 2003; Bruckert, 2002; Lewis and Maticka-Tyndale, 2000.

17 On this topic see Gillies, 2013; Love 2013; van der Meulen, 2010; van der Meulen and Durisin, 2008; HIV/AIDS Legal Network, 2006; Childs et al., 2006; Lewis et al., 2005; Bruckert, Parent, and Robitaille, 2002; Lowman, 2000, 1998, 1986.

18 See for example Currie and Gillies, 2006; May et al., 2000; McKeganey and Barnard, 1996.

19 See contributions in van der Meulen, Durisin, and Love, 2013. See also the testimony of sex workers at the Parliamentary Subcommittee on Solicitation Laws (SSLR, 2006).

20 This is also the rationale behind the production of the community booklet *Managing your work*.

21 See Bruckert, 2014 for a discussion about community-academic engagement.

22 We did not, of course, consult about analysis or findings – to do so would risk skewing the results.

23 In an effort to "give back to the community" we produced an open access report (Bruckert and Law, 2013) and a widely distributed community product entitled *Managing Sex Work* (Clamen, Bruckert, and Mensah, 2013).

24 Participants in both the individual and focus-group interviews were invited to select their own pseudonyms; however, to ensure anonymity, they were advised not to select their work, street, or nick names.

25 This broad definition is consistent with the framing in New Zealand, where the authority of "lower-level" managers such as receptionists is recognized (Mossman, 2010; see also Jeffrey, this collection).

26 Individuals who had been interviewed in phase one were not allowed to participate in phase two.

27 Focus groups were conducted in Ottawa (3 groups, 6 participants), Toronto (4 groups, 25 participants), Montreal (1 group, 7 participants) and Halifax (2 groups, 14 participants).

28 See Shaver (2005) for a discussion on the challenges of researching the sex industry.

29 See Goffman (1963) for the seminal work on symbolic stigma. Structural stigma is defined by Stacey Hannem (2012) as arising out of an *awareness* of the problematic attributes of a particular group of people and is based on an intent to manage a population that is perceived, on the basis of the stigmatic attribute, to be "risky" or morally bereft ... The stigma is *structural* because the difficulties that arise from it are not so much a product of the stigma itself, or any inherent problems that arise from the condition, but of the institutional and conceptual structures that surround it ... The individual is marked and may be subject to a myriad of interventions, regulations, and surveillance, not on the basis of *individual* factors, but on the recognition that he or she belongs to a statistically "risky" group (Hannem, 2012, 24).

1 The Representation of the "Pimp": A Barrier to Understanding the Work of Third Parties in the Adult Canadian Sex Industry

MARIA NENGEH MENSAH[1]

\pimp\

1. *Noun.* A criminal who is associated with, usually exerts control over, and lives off the earnings of one or more prostitutes. Origin: Probably akin to British dialect *pimp* small bundle of sticks, Middle English *pymple* papule, German *Pimpf* young boy, kid, literally, little fart, *Pumpf*. First Known Use: 1701

2. *Verb.* To get customers for prostitutes. *Transitive verb (slang):* To make use of often dishonorably for one's own gain or benefit. *Intransitive verb* to work as a pimp.

– Merriam-Webster's Dictionary and Thesaurus, 2015

Drawing on examples from popular culture and from an original Canadian news archive, this chapter examines how representations of the "pimp" are used to talk about third party involvement in sex work. I suggest that two processes are discernable in the current discourse about procuring and "pimping": in contrast to the very negative framing of the work of "pimps" in the press, popular culture regularly offers a more optimistic representation of persons who control, supervise, facilitate, and/or coordinate the labour of those in the commercial sex industry. Press representations, often infused with gender and race markers, are powerful social constructs – the building blocks of a contemporary discourse on sexual dishonour and punishment, and at the same time, an obstacle to effectively understanding the work of organizers, receptionists, promoters, agents, middle-persons, service providers, drivers, and managers of sex workers.

On Representation and Common Sense

According to Stuart Hall (1997) representation is "the process by which members of a culture use language (broadly defined as any system which deploys signs, any signifying system) to produce meaning" (61). This definition carries an important premise about the social construction of things, objects, people, and events: their meaning will always change from one culture or period to another. Hall (1997) explains that the practice of representation involves forging links between what we might refer to broadly as "the world of things, people, events and experience" – in short the conceptual world – and the signs, arranged into languages, which "stand for" or communicate these concepts (61). Therefore representations of the "pimp" and "pimping" make sense for us because they draw on lived experience and recognizable situations, and we associate them with concepts and symbols that allow us to talk about third party management in the adult sex industry.

Furthermore, Hall (1997) uses the notion of "common sense" to explain the work of representation in the everyday. He shows that the spontaneous and shared character of common-sense knowledge makes it seem neutral and transparent. Yet, it is the intuitive quality of common sense about something that creates a barrier to effectively knowing that thing:

It is precisely its "spontaneous" quality, its transparency, its "naturalness," its refusal to be made to examine the premises on which it is founded, its resistance to change or to correction, its effect of instant recognition, and the closed circle in which it moves which makes common sense, at one and the same time, "spontaneous," ideological and unconscious. (Hall, 1979, 325)

For Hall, nothing new can be learned from common sense. This mode of communication only allows us to see how things are in the established order and system. We take common sense for granted and render its premises invisible. It follows that in order to study how common sense shapes our knowledge of third parties in the sex industry as "pimps," we must first look at how popular culture constructs these representations, and makes apparent their underpinnings. To do so we reflect on the array of cultural products that exist around the figure of the "pimp." Rap and hip-hop music, Halloween costumes, films, music videos, TV shows, and auto/biographies forge a popular representation of the "pimp" (Boyd, 1997; Quinn, 2000).

The "Pimp" in Popular Culture

The noun "pimp" seems to have first appeared in English over three hundred years ago and was used then as now to mean a person who arranges opportunities for sexual encounters with a prostitute and (usually) exerts control over their earnings. The verb *to pimp* dates from the early seventeenth century, but the word has seen a contemporary revival of sorts with media attention to – and glamorization of – the "inner-city pimp." In the 1970s, for example, terms such as "pimpmobile"[2] and "pimp walk"[3] were introduced in Blaxploitation films. Indeed, this genre of films tended to take place in the "ghetto" and involve drug dealing and petty crimes, often with stereotyped depiction of Blacks as poor and criminal. In many ways, it has created a very specific image of the Black male "pimp" who wears fur coats and hats.[4] More recently, we have seen the advent of a range of non-sexual figurative uses. We can now "pimp" our possessions, making them flashy, decorated, or customized, as in MTV's car-detailing show, *Pimp My Ride.*[5]

The language we use is testament to how we, in North America, have collectively appropriated the term to talk about different situations. In fact, the term *pimp* is often used in everyday vernacular outside the context of commercial sex. This is the case with the emergence of web series such as the Québec program *Pimp My Garage*:

> In *Pimp My Garage*, Frédéric Charpentier teams up with the designer Emilia Cerretti and handymen to renovate messy garages into impressive spaces that will make you drool with envy: bar, music room, hangout for guys, and more! With the gang of *Pimp My Garage*, you can expect dramatic changes, but also lots of fun![6]

Here the word *pimp* is used to refer to the improvement of a thing, a service, or a situation. The web series *Felipé, The Sausage Pimp* is another example of this use of the term: the figure of the "pimp" presents an opportunity to differentiate Felipé Saint-Laurent from other sausage makers; it is a distinctive quality that makes him stand out professionally. Portrayed as a traditional craftsman, Felipé's online cooking show is extremely popular. "We follow in his creative delirium, his collaborations with major chefs, his tribulations and his unusual way of creating great gastronomic events!"[7] The series highlights for viewers the inner workings of the sausage-manufacturing business from the point of view of the cook-hustler. As Staiger (2005) puts it:

The notion of the pimp as hustler echoes American values on a broader scale, in which moral worth is often measured in terms of economic success and captured in such phrases as "making it" or "being a loser." Valuing those who show entrepreneurship and healthy egotism … this moral value system is still envisioned as a primarily male endeavour where the man is the breadwinner of the family, as economic success and independence are critical facets of hegemonic manhood. (423)

Such positive representations of the "pimp" persona, however, are not dominant in our popular culture. More commonly, "pimp culture" is the umbrella term through which we map the interlocking systems of oppression that create material conditions under which women experience bodily and psychological harm from men. To understand the nature of this more negative image of the "pimp" is to recognize the importance of gender as well as style in business and popular culture (Anderson, 1999; Kochman, 1981). As we saw in the Introduction, in the "pimp-prostitute" dyad, the media ascribes to women the role of victim and men the role of "pimp." Women are represented as being abused and having low self-esteem. Men are represented as aggressive exploiters. In so doing, the link to concepts such as gender and sexual equality is articulated for readers. This representation opens up a very critical analysis of the cultural products that glamorize and commodify the "pimping lifestyle" (Gelder, 2007; Schmitt, 2013). As Bell and Ward (2013) write on their blog: "Pimp culture employs white supremacy, misogyny, racism, homophobia and the dogma of rugged individualism to physically and psychically undermine our sense of self, diminishing our capacity for self-determination." Indeed, if there is a detested figure, it is that the male "pimp."

News Coverage of "Pimping" Subcultures

According to Jeffrey and MacDonald (2006), journalistic coverage of criminal cases involving "pimps" are marked by dehumanizing myths about sex, gender, and ethnicity. Their unique study of the Halifax *Chronicle Herald's* reporting of the dismantling of a "prostitution ring" in Halifax and Toronto in 1992, found that the media created a moral panic. Using hyper-dramatic terminology and sensational narrative tropes, news articles depicted "white girls" who were "abducted" by "Black men," subjected to painful beatings and death threats, forced into selling sex, and then taken to other places in Canada or the United States. These horrific accounts subsequently justified stricter control of women's movements (through more restrictions on sexual behaviour) and that of non-white men (through new immigration laws). In this news coverage, for which the authors coined the term *pimping panic*, popular press and police discourses combined to define the common-sense knowledge of the "pimp" at the same time as they facilitated the public designation of this as a significant threat to the values and interests of Canadian society. Similarly, in her study of how the Canadian news media represents racialized groups, Jiwani (2011) argues that stereotypes are part of common-sense knowledge. According to her, the media communicates racism by inviting the public to support the criminalization of particular communities and groups. Jeffrey and MacDonald (2006) come to the same conclusion, writing "the media are central players in choosing whose story is told and how and, therefore, how the public in general perceives the issue of the sex trade" (147).[8]

Building on this body of work, we reviewed the news coverage between 2000 and 2010 in two English-language national newspapers, the *Globe and Mail* and the *National Post*, as well as two French-language dailies, *La Presse* and *Le Soleil*. Our goal was not to do an exhaustive content analysis of the media coverage but to glimpse how "pimps" are represented and to sort out the main themes in common knowledge about them. A decade of newspaper clippings were collected using keyword searches in electronic media databases. Thousands of articles containing the word *pimp* or *proxén** were archived. From this, a small sample of two hundred articles was selected for qualitative content analysis using NVivo®. Article selection for the corpus was based on the following criteria: the article must be about Canada or have a direct Canadian connection, and it must be about lived experiences involving the practices of sex industry third parties as defined by the Management Project.[9] The analytical codes included reference details (date and location of the article); sources and their positioning; the content of the article (including context, legal, organizational, economic, cultural, and social aspects); the issues involved (e.g., labour, race, and women's issues); the discourses being produced about management, sex workers, the sex industry, and criminalization; and the effects of these discourses, including the problems and solutions they put forth. Prevalent stereotypes, discourses, and peaks in news coverage were also noted.

Our review revealed that a majority of articles where the keyword *pimp* (English) or *proxén** (French) appeared were published in the main news section of the paper. "Pimp" was on the front page about twenty times in the decade of news reports, which suggests that "pimping" is a subject of interest for readers and that the newspapers reviewed perceived it to be a relevant topic that would sell papers. The bulk of articles featuring third parties, usually male "pimps" at the street level, detailed raids or rescues, arrests, charges being laid, and/or court processes. As such, most of these articles were informed by law enforcement. Always depicted as criminals, "pimps" were also described as recruiters, child abusers, or abusive and manipulative boyfriends.[10] Female third parties and madams appeared very seldom.[11]

Locating the "Pimp"

Given that most readers have little contact with the sex industry, news coverage plays a significant role in shaping public understanding of who the "pimp" is, where and with whom he operates, and what experiences are associated with his (generally deemed illegal) activities. In this sense newspaper articles provide readily available depictions of things, people, events, and experiences. In the next section we examine the ensuing connections to the conceptual worlds of the adult sex industry; location; gangsterism; violence; and human trafficking.

Location in the Adult Sex Industry

The first representation of the male "pimp" is related to the sector of the adult sex industry. Most articles mention cities in Ontario and Québec and describe massage parlours, strip clubs, escort agencies, street-based prostitution, law, and court hearings. While some articles are about escort agencies – depicted in a surprisingly banal manner – there were few articles about brothels per se. Instead the terms *brothel* or *bawdy house* were employed in relation to charges laid at strip clubs and massage parlours. At the same time, news representations of strip club managers largely reflected the ambiguity of prevailing popular and legal opinions about strip clubs, which ranged from established (i.e., tolerable if not legitimate) community businesses to spaces of exploitation. Strip club managers voiced their objections, both collectively and individually, to changes in foreign exotic dancer visas in 2004, in what was dubbed "Strippergate" when immigration minister Judy Sgro was accused of fast tracking the visa renewal of a Romanian stripper who had worked on her re-election campaign (CP, 2004a). In contrast to other types of "pimps," the managers of escort agencies were represented as belonging to a higher social class. For example, one agency owner is described as a "pleasure consultant" and the "chief executive officer" of the business (Ray, 2002).

Gangsterism

A second significant representation of the "pimp" takes place in the space of gangsterism. There was some variability in how these organized crime groups were presented. For example the Hells Angels were mentioned as having taken control of several strip clubs in Ontario, not to exploit women but rather to distribute drugs: "They have been buying rundown hotels in centres between Montreal and Toronto to fix up as strip clubs, a serious business in itself and even more so as a way to distribute drugs" (Cameron, 2002). While the Hells Angels were depicted as institutional, professional, and organized, other gangs were associated with the sale of girls for money and drugs (White and Meaney, 2007). One *biker* told the journalist outright that he does not appreciate media representations that associate gangs with criminals:

> The Hells Angels are part and parcel of the American dream. It's like joining the top group in the world. It's a complex and interesting organization, just to meet the different members. But you journalists never write about the Hells Angel who plays in an orchestra or the ones who are computer programmers. (Cameron, 2002)

That said, in the coverage of a Québec juvenile prostitution ring involving up to thirty girls, a gang called the Wolf Pack was alleged to have paid some of their prostitution-derived profits to the Hells Angels who controlled the area (Séguin, 2002, 2003). In this ring, the man in charge of recruiting posed as a clairvoyant and had a 1-900 number for his services, while another man involved ran an art store as a front. Gang members recruited teenaged girls – some of whom were from "middle class families" while others were "runaways" or otherwise vulnerable (living at group homes, for example) – at malls and other public places frequented by young people (Hanes, 2002b).[12] One article makes sure to highlight the unspeakable character of the menacing "gangster pimp":

> Quebec City's top radio host and several prominent businessmen have been arrested in a crackdown on a juvenile prostitution ring that has become the talk of the city ... "These girls could be your daughters," Quebec City police captain André Filion said at a news conference yesterday. "Most come from good families and were recruited at school, in shopping malls, arcades and hip-hop parties" ... According to police, the ring employed girls who could each earn as much $2,000 a week for their pimps. "The pimps kept most of the money," Mr. Filion said, insisting that

minors were requested by clients to "perform sexual acts that were out of the ordinary and that surpass the imagination." He refused to give details of the specific sexual acts. (Hanes, 2002a)

Another gang that attracted much media attention was the North Preston's Finest, from Nova Scotia (Mandel, 2007). The gang was comprised of about fifty racialized men who lured "teenaged women into prostitution" by posing as their boyfriends, tattooed themselves and "their girls," and were allegedly involved in domestic trafficking, violence, and murder.[13]

> Although evidence presented in court is prohibited from being published, police in Ontario and Nova Scotia previously alleged all four of the accused were either members or had ties to the North Preston Finest, a Halifax-area gang suspected of being involved in transporting women from the East Coast to Ontario and other provinces where they are allegedly forced into working in the sex trade as either prostitutes or exotic dancers.
>
> At the time their arrest warrants were issued, police said the gang had been known to use fear and violence against young women to force them to work in the sex trade.
>
> In addition to being charged with kidnapping and sexual assault, all four accused have also been charged with forcible confinement, gang sexual assault, assault, destroying or withholding documents and human trafficking. (Mitchel, 2007)

Moreover, if not explicitly linked to gangs, "pimps" were sometimes described as connected to organized crime networks or families. International gangs, especially from Eastern Europe, were mentioned in relation to trafficking and strip clubs.

Sadistic Acts of Violence

A third representation of the male "pimp" evokes sadistic acts of violence against women. "Pimps" were described as "predators who lured young women, teenagers, and runaways into prostitution," convincing them with flattery or elaborate courtship, which experts referred to as "love-bombing" (Dorais and Corriveau, 2009), by buying them nice things and/ or drugs, or with the allure of cash. However, "pimps" are also represented as individuals who "beat their women," or control them through threats of violence to themselves or to their families. In one case, a "pimp" controlled a woman by kidnapping her young child for six weeks (Leong, 2009). The articles about Gabriel Patterson and his accomplices are exemplary in this regard: they are characterized by graphic depictions of violent acts that seem to surpass the task of informing readers. We learn that victims are "burned, beaten, threatened with gruesome mutilation and forced to perform a degrading sexual act" (Gadd, 2000, 2001).

Many articles describe "pimps" who were also the women's boyfriends (MacDonald, 2004), and some report teenagers forcing other teenagers into prostitution, including a fourteen-year-old girl being "manipulated by a younger [thirteen-year-old], tougher girl" (CP, 2004b). One case involved three adults kidnapping an eleven-year-old girl, transporting her from the United States to Canada, and keeping her in a hotel, awake on drugs, working twelve-hour stints. In another case, two escort agency security guards murdered two escorts, allegedly to steal their money (Appleby, 2000). The press provides details of the extremely cruel attitude and behaviour these *sadistic* "pimps" display towards sex workers:

> District attorney Nancy Westveld seemed equally confident. "We have all our ducks in a row," she said. "Defendants always think that prostitutes don't matter and that when they hurt them or kill them, they will somehow get a pass. That isn't what's happening here" … Both young women were shot twice in the head with a .38 revolver, trussed up with sheets and electrical cord and dumped like garbage a few blocks from the house where they were killed. And, almost as appalling, the very men who were paid to protect them are accused of killing them. (Appleby, 2000)

Human Trafficking

Finally, reports of extreme violence permeate articles about human trafficking, where the trafficker is collapsed into the figure of the male "pimp." In effect, as noted in the Introduction, the term *trafficker* is increasingly used as another word for "pimp." Indeed, traffickers were often depicted as deceiving poor women about the jobs they would be doing in the destination country, either wholly or in part. In these stories, the women were sometimes taken directly to Canada, while other times they were shipped around to several countries, or bought and sold several times between agents. After they arrived, the women were handed over to "local agents" who held their passports and forced them to repay a debt by working as prostitutes and/or strippers for long periods with almost no days off. These agents kept the women's money and often also sexually assaulted them. Traffickers also threatened the women's families directly or indirectly so as to "control the woman" (Jimenez, 2000a). In some stories, women were sold by traffickers, usually to massage parlours, and forced to work off their debt while their passports and other documents were confiscated. In a case covered in several articles in May 2001, a Thai woman was sold for $15,000 (Jimenez, 2000b). Narratives about young women who escape from "being trafficked" provide another viewpoint from which the "pimp" is vilified in the press:

> Alison planned her escape carefully, filling her canvas tote bag with jeans, street shoes and a heavy sweater. She hid them in her locker at the suburban strip club where she worked, alongside her slinky dresses and long black boots. On her final day as a "sex slave," she brought along her Lion King toy and a yellow stuffed bird for luck. Then, the petite 25-year-old made a dash for freedom … Alison feared the agents who had brought her from Budapest to Toronto to work as a "burlesque entertainer" would track her down and force her to finish her six-month contract. "I was scared. I wanted to give myself up but I didn't know who to trust," she recalls. (Jimenez, 2000b)

Domestic trafficking, wherein "pimps" moved their workers around the country or sold them to other "pimps" in different cities, was addressed, but generally speaking Canada was described as a destination for trafficking. For example, Freeze (2010) reports "a flourishing and clandestine trade in sexual services – from the Asian massage parlours operating in B.C.'s Lower Mainland to the Eastern European escort agencies based in Toronto and Montreal." The French-language newspaper *La Presse* insists: "The City of Vancouver is becoming a favorite place for child-sex tourists"[14] (Sirois, 2003).

Association with gangs, violence, sadistic behaviour, and human trafficking defines the "pimp" not only as a misogynistic manipulator but also as "a performance that allows positioning oneself more generally as in control, rather than being controlled" (Staiger, 2005, 425).

Sources and Credibility

In the face of such powerful representations it is imperative to reflect upon journalistic practices, including examining which social actors reporters rely upon for their information (Baron 2006). The distribution of credibility through journalists' reliance on certain sources over others reflects, and arguably reinforces, the stigma against some sources, namely here the "pimp" him/herself. Based on a subsample of our two-hundred-article news archive (those published in the *Globe and Mail* between 2000 and 2010), police were overwhelmingly consulted.[15] In addition, in articles in which only one source was cited, it was almost always law enforcement. The exception to this was in one-on-one interviews with sex workers (often referred to as "call girls" or "strippers") or managers/owners (most often of strip clubs). This may come as no surprise given the news outlets' overt reliance on dominant social, legal, and political institutions for quotes, and the wide range of organizational constraints on journalists, such as tight deadlines, space or time limitations, and the need to determine newsworthiness (Ericson et al., 1987).

The degree to which representatives from the community and local businesses outnumbered those from the sex industry also suggests that sex workers and "pimps" are seen as comparatively less reliable or important sources. Indeed, Goffman (1963) identifies stigma as precisely this *dis*credibility. This is indicative of the fact that the adult sex industry is represented as the problem (either in the justice system or at the community level) about which the police and community members are consulted with an eye to finding a solution.

In this context strip club management appeared to be granted the most legitimacy as a sex industry source, both in terms of description and frequency of citations. With respect to the former, strip club personnel were more likely to be described as jobholders with particular responsibilities, such as "manager," "president," "owner," or "bouncer," as opposed to managers in other sectors of the adult sex industry who were represented, for the most part, as stereotypes ("sadistic pimp") or caricatures (the "Mansion Madam") (Patrick, 2007). Moreover, strip club personnel were identified in a range of ways, from giving their first and last names and titles to, less often, being anonymous sources. Terry Koumoudouros, owner of the club House of Lancaster in Toronto and also head of his local business association, was featured nominally in a variety of articles and even photographed (Dale, 2007; Hachey, 2004).

Conceptual Worlds: Criminalization and Racial Stereotyping

As other research has noted, there is a consistency in the media representation of the "pimp" as "more negatively portrayed than prostitutes" (Stenvoll, 2002, 149). Much has been written on the stigma against sex workers (Shaver, Lewis, and Maticka-Tyndale, 2011; Hannem and

Bruckert, 2014; Lazarus et al., 2012; Pheterson, 1996), which is deep-seated and ingrained in the *Criminal Code of Canada* (Lowman, 2000). Yet little is known about the actual work that "pimps" do in the sex industry. Although our analysis is limited to representations of the "pimp," we would now like to question what other aspects of third party work are bound up with these representations in such a way that the term *pimp* acts as a blinder or an obstacle preventing access to knowledge about the various other kinds of third party work in the sex industry, and other meanings we can derive from them.

What we know of the "pimp" from the news is profoundly negative. We are provided with information that the "pimp" is the enemy, the predator, the threat. By common-sense standards, he is dangerous and responsible for violent and aggressive acts. Two major analytical concepts come to mind to extract the meaning of these representations of the "pimp": criminality and racial stereotyping.

First, as noted earlier, the content of the articles in our news archive is overwhelmingly about crimes committed by "pimps" and their associates: economic exploitation, physical violence, sexual abuse, attempted murder, kidnapping, sexual harassment, or other problematic sexual conduct. "Pimps" are represented as destructive, "evil," and amoral. Newspapers also warn us that "pimping" is exacerbated at times of large sporting events, such as the Super Bowl, the World Cup, the Olympics, and Formula One races.[16] If criminalization is to render particular behaviour illegal, to transform the individual into a criminal or treat them as such, then this is precisely what journalistic representations accomplish by identifying "pimping" as dangerous to the dominant social order and designating it as criminally punishable. In addition, given the high credibility accorded to law-enforcement sources, readers are encouraged to adopt a punitive stance. "Pimping" is to be punished, and we are informed about how law and order can return as quickly as possible. This has been an important function of news media historically (Ericson et al., 1987),[17] and this is still very much the case. In the recent Ottawa "teen pimp" saga discussed in the Introduction, the *Ottawa Sun* gleefully reported that "[Judge] Lahaie showed her [the alleged "ring leader"] the same mercy the girl showed to her victims – six in all – piling up convictions with the ruthless efficiency of a pool shark on a hot run." When the young woman, who was fifteen at the time of the offence, received a severe adult sentence the justice system was praised for making the "right decision" (see Seymour, 2015).

Second, news representations of the "pimp" are also notable for racial stereotyping and stigmatic marking. This occurs in journalistic descriptions that range from depictions of young Black males convicted of crimes to reports of racial profiling, and various analyses and critiques thereof. The coverage surrounding Adonis Stevenson, the Québec boxing champion born in Haiti, is one example of the complex ways racial stereotyping plays out in the news. When he defended his world champion title for the second time in 2013, rather than focus on his skills in the ring the media "remembered" and accentuated the fact that he had previously served a four-year sentence for "pimping, assault and threats to 17 to 25 year old prostitutes" (CP, 2000). In addition, the press emphasized that Stevenson did not express remorse for the crimes he committed and many of his victims were quoted about the violence he inflicted. This type of coverage suggests that if you've once been a "pimp," you're always a "pimp." It is an indelible mark (Hannem and Bruckert, 2014).

Moreover, the Adonis coverage is also interesting for the way in which racism was explicitly addressed in some articles. Apparently, after his opponent had insulted him at a press conference, Stevenson called him and the media racist: "It's a sentence that goes back seventeen years so why is it still on the front page? When I do something positive, like now, no one talks about it. That's racism!" (Béland, 2013). Stevenson's remark, quoted in the press and later on television, speaks to the news media's inability to widely disseminate alternative representations of the "pimp." A Black boxer (always) has the conceptual likelihood (because of his gender, his race, his ability, and his class) of acting like/being a "pimp":

> The assumption that Black men's heterosexual encounters are all based upon this kind of manipulation and instrumental behaviour is not only racist in and of itself; it also serves to reinforce other popular racist ideas about both Black men and women, as well as to police "interracial" sexual relationships. In the same way that white racism constructs pimps as Black men and Black men as pimps, ideologies which "Otherize" prostitute women make it impossible to distinguish between pimps and boyfriends. (O'Connell, 1998, 44)

Much has been written on the racism embedded in the representation of the Black "pimp," especially in the United States, where most of the "pimp" autobiographical work and other products of popular culture – including Blaxploitation films – historically originate (Gelder, 2007; Jackson, 2006). For example, Robert "Iceberg Slim" Beck, a "pimp" for twenty-five years who went on to become a writer of bestselling paperbacks, was very influential among African American readers, hip-hop artists, and rappers. His legacy of outlandish clothing, fast cars, his jazz-loving character, and his rags-to-riches story remain uniquely American (Gifford, 2015). Despite his commercial success, though, with respect to his relationships to sex workers and to women more generally, Iceberg Slim was also described as – and proclaimed himself to be – a manipulative Black man (Slim, 1967).

Concluding Reflections

In this chapter, we suggest that the "pimp" is a powerful social construct set up by popular and journalistic representations that fix the meaning of the word *pimp* in the sex industry in two distinct ways. First, popular culture offers generally positive representations of savvy persons as stylish, cool, and shrewd business operators who are able to transform anything into a moneymaking scheme. Second, news media rely on a negative image of the "pimp" as a male tyrant who profits from coercing his female victims into prostitution. He is often racialized as a Black "pimp." This is "the intolerable nature" of the "pimp" "against which humanity rises" (Foucart, 2011). Located in every sector of the adult sex industry, with a few exceptions (the managers of escort agencies or strip clubs), "pimps" are described as recruiters, child abusers, violent and manipulative boyfriends, and human traffickers. Female third parties and madams are rarely mentioned. The emphasis is on criminality and racial stereotyping.

Insofar as the representation of the "pimp" is a fixture in the present Canadian cultural landscape, the degree to which popular and journalistic depictions characterize "pimps" requires a deeper analysis of the relationship between the activities of third parties involved in the adult sex industry – a culture in its own right – and the representation of that culture. The coming chapters map what third parties do, who they are, and who they work with, while avoiding the pitfalls inherent to the conflation of sex work managers and "pimps." This, I hope, can go a long way toward filling the need for empirical research that goes beyond discourse and stereotypical representations.

Notes

1 The author wishes to acknowledge the research assistants whose work made this chapter possible: Tuulia Law, Geneviève Dauphin-Johnson, Michael Chacha Enriquez, and Myriam Pomerleau. Thank you.

2 "Pimpmobiles" became part of popular culture when they were depicted in 1970s "Blaxploitation" films that targeted the urban Black audience with Black actors at the forefront and soundtracks of funk and soul music. In that context, it is the name for the vehicle that a "pimp" drives.

3 A "pimp walk" is a sort of gendered swaggering or "an ostentatious style of walking affected by men wishing to assert their dominance" (Wojcik, 2010). It is a form of machismo or sexual display, which takes up more space than needed for simple motion. It is also known as a "jive-ass walk" and a cane may be used as a walking stick as part of the performance.

4 Some of the most popular Blaxploitation movies include *Black Caesar* (Cohen, 1973), *Dolemite* (Martin, 1975), *The Mack* (Poole, 1973), *Willie Dynamite* (Moses, 1974), Gordon Parks' Black detective trilogy *Shaft* (1971), *Shaft's Big Score!* (1972), and *Shaft in Africa* (1973), as well as a series of films featuring former Black football stars (such as Fred Williamson and Jim Brown) and the actress Pam Grier; these include *Coffy* (Hill, 1973), *Black Mama, White Mama* (Romero, 1973), *Foxy Brown* (Hill, 1974), and *Sheba Baby* (Gerdler, 1975). All show both the attraction and the detrimental aspects of the "pimping" lifestyle.

5 *Pimp My Ride* has enjoyed worldwide popularity and has been translated into many different languages for publics in Canada, Germany, Italy, New Zealand, Brazil, and countries throughout the Middle East. An episode generally begins with the participant showing his or her car off, and convincing MTV why it needs to be "pimped." The host shows up at the participant's house, takes a look at the car himself, makes wisecracks about the particular things that are wrong with it, and promises the owner a complete makeover. Each car is a custom "pimp," tailored to the personalities and interests of the owners. At the end of the show, the improved car is revealed to its owner, as well as all the details of the renovation and the custom features.

6 Translated passage. See http://www.canalvie.com/emissions/pimp-mon -garage-1.1216653.

7 Translated passage. See http://www.zeste.tv/emissions/felipe-le-pimp -de-la-saucisse/.

8 See Ferris (2015) for a recent analysis of dominant sex worker tropes in the media.

9 Individuals who work (or worked) as third parties in various sectors of the sex industry (street-based, incall, outcall, and strip clubs) in the Maritimes, Québec, and Ontario since 2000. See also Introduction, this collection.

10 The most detailed story about "pimping" was that of Gabriel Patterson, extensively covered and gruesomely described in national and provincial newspapers between 2000 and 2002 (CP, 2002).

11 For some, the idea that there were a few articles reporting on women as "pimps" may seem counterintuitive, since they are so rare and do not "make sense" given that we are used to reading about "pimps" as men. Our news corpus generated three articles about Canadian-born stripper Lisa Ann Taylor, the so-called Mansion Madam accused of running a brothel out of her million-dollar home in the United States. The press reports that she pleaded guilty to several charges, and has been sentenced to seven years of probation (AP, 2008; Hall, 2007; Patrick, 2007).

12 Here again we see the tendency of coverage to simultaneously exceptionalize and normalize the population "at risk."

13 As noted above, Jeffrey and MacDonald (2006) have written extensively on this coverage in terms of the "pimping panic."

14 Translated headline.

15 In detail, for these two hundred articles, the sources most commonly cited were police (102); individual community members and non-profit organizations (60); lawyers, both crown and others (60); strip-club owners and managers (47); federal government officials (35); local business owners (32); academics (20); provincial government officials (26); strippers (18); other sex workers (18); municipal government officials (12); clients (6); "pimps" (3); and "madams" (1).

16 Julie Ham (2011) shows that there is no evidence that large sporting events increase trafficking for prostitution. However, despite the lack of evidence, this idea continues to hold great appeal for prohibitionist groups, anti-immigration groups, politicians, and journalists. According to Ham, "the resilience of this inaccurate claim could be due to: Its usefulness as a fundraising strategy; its effectiveness in grabbing the media and the public's attention; being a quick, easy way to be seen 'doing something' about trafficking; being a more socially acceptable guise for prostitution abolitionist agendas and anti-immigration agendas." (9).

17 In their book *Visualizing Deviance: A Study of News Organisation*, Ericson et al. (1987) empirically demonstrated that the news on crime, deviance, and control forms an integral part of news reporting. In fact, according to these authors, reporting on crimes is particularly well suited to the enhancement of the media's primary role: policing of organizational life and reaffirming

its moral boundaries. The imagery of "pimp"-related criminality, then, not only helps to accentuate the norm ("pimps" are bad and should be punished), but also promotes a vision of society capable of constant self-evaluation and self-correction (what are the police doing about it?).

2 Who Are Third Parties? Pathways In and Out of Third Party Work

CHRIS BRUCKERT

In the previous chapter, "The Representation of the 'Pimp,' " Maria Nengeh Mensah examined the "common-sense" narratives about third parties perpetuated in the media. She noted that these representations – resplendent with highly gendered and racialized images of sex industry third parties as "pimps," traffickers, dangerous criminals, evil predators, or at a minimum callous, creepy bosses, and/or abusive partners – reflect, reproduce, and affirm the normative framing found in Canadian laws, and in the assertions of Conservative Party politicians and neo-prohibitionists. When we juxtapose these caricatures to the complex reality that emerged when we spoke with sex workers and third parties, the extent to which they are based on generalizations, stereotypes, and stigmatic assumptions comes into sharp relief. We see, for example, that in striking contrast to the prevailing trope, third party work in the sex industry is largely women's work (this is true in both outcall and incall establishments and on the street, although notably not the case for strip clubs).[1] Moreover, on the street and in the incall/outcall sector the line between sex worker and third party is exceptionally porous, rendering the sharp distinction between sex workers (as victims) and third parties (as predators) spurious. As we will see in the coming pages, these roles frequently overlap, and sometimes alternate, as individuals navigate their personal and professional obligations within the options at their disposal. Given that our social world is characterized by the unequal distribution of social, economic, and personal capital, "choices" are inevitably constrained by socio-structural factors (e.g., class, ethnicity) as well as personal characteristics (e.g., skills, competencies).

It also becomes increasingly evident that the relationships between third parties and sex workers is much more complicated and variable than the prevailing narrative of third parties exercising excessive authority and control over sex workers (see also Benoit et al., 2014). Indeed it is more appropriate to think about a spectrum of relationships between sex workers and the individuals who supervise, control, facilitate, and/or coordinate their labour process and/or practices. Indeed sometimes – when the third party is a contractor or freelance worker who is hired by independent sex workers or agencies and paid on a fee-for-service or shift rate to provide specific services or clusters of services – the power relations are inverted: it is the sex worker who hires and establishes expectations. For indoor workers these services might include receptionist duties, transportation, and web support, while in strip clubs they would be the drivers. In the outdoor sector these contractors are, generally speaking, other street-involved individuals who, in exchange for a small fee paid in cash or sometimes in drugs, provide either business services (e.g., procuring clients, providing a work space) or security (e.g., recording licence plate numbers, accompanying sex workers, providing security in the parking lots where sex workers take their clients). In a context where, as research has clearly demonstrated, sex workers are particularly vulnerable to predatory violence at the same time as real and perceived bias restricts their access to police protection (Bruckert and Chabot, 2010; Jeffrey and MacDonald, 2006; Lowman, 2000), these third parties may well be providing a vital service.

Other third parties are associates in symbiotic and mutually beneficial relationships with sex workers. This category includes, for example, agents, event planners, and worksite providers who *work with* sex workers: disc jockeys in strip clubs would fall under this classification, as would mentors for incall/outcall workers; on the street, as we will see later in this chapter, drug dealers might sometimes be categorized in this way as well (see Gillies and Bruckert, 2018). Finally, some third parties conform to the "classic" (or agency) model: third parties who engage sex workers. In these cases there is a much more explicit hierarchy, one that sometimes resembles an employee-employer relationship to the extent that third parties "hire" sex workers and exercise a measure of control over their labour process and practices (e.g., hours of work, expectations regarding attire). It is important to appreciate that these relationships are further complicated when, as is sometimes the case, sex workers are in intimate relationships with individuals who are also their third parties. As is the case for an estimated 4 per cent of Canadian women (Centre for Justice Statistics, 2016),[2] these relationships are sometimes characterized by

emotional, physical, sexual, and/or financial abuse – the markers of intimate partner violence.

In this sense we can appreciate that power relations between sex
workers and third parties are complex, layered, and conditioned not
only by social, structural, and personal factors but also by where on
the spectrum the particular relationship falls and whether there is a
personal as well as professional component.[3] As we see throughout this
collection, for the most part, third parties provide for a cost (ranging
from minimal to reasonable to excessive) services that sex workers find
beneficial, including such things as security, a place to see clients, business support, and training. As is the case in other labour sectors, when
a worker's circumstances change, or the quality/reliability of the third
party's services decline, or when the costs outweigh the benefits, sex
workers terminate the relationship.

This chapter draws on the Management Project's[4] interviews with 75
sex industry third parties from the incall/outcall (50), street (12), and
strip club (13) sectors to consider: who are the people who supervise,
control, facilitate, and/or coordinate the work of sex workers? Our
demographics immediately challenge gendered and racialized tropes:
48 research participants were women (including 2 trans women) while
27 were men.[5] Gender representation was sector specific: men dominated in strip clubs (all 13 participants were male), while on the street
this was the case for only 4 participants; 10 incall/outcall third parties
identified as men. In terms of ethnicity the majority (43) were white,
while 6 identified as Black, 2 as Asian, 2 as Indigenous, 2 as "mixed," 2
as "Aboriginal and Black," 2 as "half Native and half Caucasian," one
as "Native and French," and one participant said she was "a woman
of colour."[6] Our sample varied widely in terms of age and experience;
ages ranged from 24 to 62 years (with an average age of 40) and from 3
months to 40 years of experience working as a third party. Thirty-two
were sex workers and third parties concurrently. In short, while some
of our participants might conform to the stereotypical representation,
these were certainly not reflective of the sample as a whole.

Pathways In: Becoming a Third Party

Nuancing the demographic profile of third parties and unpacking their
relationships to sex workers destabilizes "common sense" assumptions
and stereotypes. It also raises a number of questions. Why did these
individuals, in the face of such negative narratives about "the kind of

people who are third parties," elect to do this work? What, if anything, prompted them to move into other employment? These questions, which could be asked about any other occupational group, guide the remainder of the chapter. We will see that entry into this role is usually facilitated either by sex work experience or by virtue of an individual's social, family, or work networks. Sometimes it is as simple as answering an advertisement and, very occasionally, individuals find themselves inadvertently assuming the role, albeit not necessarily the identity, of third parties.

It (Often) Starts with Sex Work

All but four of the female third parties (and five of the men) with whom we spoke were, or had been, sex workers. Five women who worked as third parties on the street are what can best be described as peer facilitators (see Gillies and Bruckert, 2018). For these women the opportunity for third party work often presented itself because of their relationships with women who, like themselves, were sex workers. Fanny, a street-based peer facilitator in Ottawa, found herself homeless after she fled an abusive relationship when she was in her forties; she soon became "involved in the sex trade on the street." She started organizing clients for other street-based sex workers, "because I was trying to be helpful. It started off slowly and not planned. You know one of the girls and then word of mouth got a few more of the girls involved, and then before I knew it, this was just part of my day." Lee, a street-based peer facilitator who was also a sex worker, provided security to other workers. Her business also came about by "word of mouth" after a friend who was "trans [and] afraid to walk, like, Queen Street because she's been gay-bashed before. So I would like, you know, walk with her, stand with her." Third parties like Lee are cognizant of the risks faced by sex workers and draw on their own experiences to ensure security: "If they [the worker and client] went in a laneway, I would go behind them because I was brutally beaten and sodomized in a laneway one time. If a guy's got no car or whatever, I would go to within hearing distance."

The move from worker to management is also evident in the indoor sex industry. In many ways this is hardly surprising – after all, it is common for people in other service-sector jobs to put their hard-earned skills to use by moving into managerial positions. Indeed this is often valourized: "Within any company or any business … when you get a promotion from within, those people are usually better at the job because they've done your job, and now they're doing their job" (Horeta, incall agency manager, Halifax). Jane, a sixty-two-year-old former sex worker who ran a Halifax brothel for nineteen years, told us: "When you've been through it and done it, you can explain things to the girls ... That's why I said, 'Okay, now it's time to open my place.'" Moreover, their sex work experience conditioned not only the decision to become a third party but also the approach they adopted in their professional capacity. Former and sometimes current sex workers who become third parties are well positioned to understand the nature and challenges of the job; they have learned harm-mitigation strategies, how to successfully run a business, and, significantly, understand "what not to do and how not to be" (Brittany, incall/outcall agency owner, Ottawa). For example, Lisa (incall agency owner/worker, Toronto) who had "been in the business a really long time" learnt that worker satisfaction ensures a pleasant work environment and is ultimately good for the bottom line. Accordingly, she "didn't have fines because I remember working under fines. I hated fines. And that would just give me an incentive to be a little shady and skim off the top, or however I could skim or scam extra money."[7] Mielle (outcall agency owner, Ottawa) said much the same thing: "I learned from my own experience of being a sex trade worker. Well, this doesn't work for me, so I won't do that. You know. That's how I learned, from being a worker myself." In other words sex work experience provides individuals with the skills and knowledge to successfully offer services to sex workers and, in the case of indoor workers, run a business. Although there is no easy way to determine who is a good third party, sex work experience was appreciated by some women like Alana, a sex worker in Ottawa, who explained: "They have first-hand knowledge of the kinds of things that we're going through. So you know about the stresses; you know what clients are like, and just the kind of expectations that go along with being an escort."

That still leaves the question: why did these individuals decide to become third parties? Here we see a wide range of motivations. Some, like Adele (outcall agency owner, Montreal) and EJ (massage parlour owner, Toronto), were frustrated with what they considered poor working conditions and/or unfair labour practices in the sex industry. As will become increasingly evident in the coming chapters, while some third parties are committed to providing a positive and safe work environment, offering fair wages, and ensuring sex workers retain control over their labour process, others are less diligent on these matters. Mielle (outcall agency owner, Ottawa) was working as an erotic dancer at age thirteen when her cousin "basically human trafficked, like, me into the prostitution ring where I was forced to work. So, I was traded into that and got out of it as I got older. And then, I worked for a couple of escort agencies." She puts it succinctly: "I decided that the way I was treated was bullshit ... I decided that I wanted to do my own escort agency ... I wanted girls to be able to work with me for themselves." Sylvia (outcall agency owner, Hamilton), a forty-two-year-old racial minority trans woman who had "worked for different people," echoed Mielle when she spoke of her frustration: "I just felt like some of them really didn't care about the sex worker ... There were so many fees." Sylvia was therefore committed to "giving women better opportunities to make money at a reasonable price." Lilith (mentor, Ottawa), who wanted to make the best use of her incall space after she "decided to tone down how many clients I was seeing," was also motivated to provide the same help she had received to someone new to the sex industry. Her description of what this mentoring looks like also highlights the skills required and the range of tactics sex workers employ to mitigate risk:

> When she first started, we did all the screening together. Every time a client would email her, every time she was about to send an email, she would call and run it through me first to make sure it was done properly. I told her that she needs to ask six questions of clients, and she needs to ask for a reference, and she needs to get a legitimate phone number and talk to them on the phone. When a client answered the questionnaire, we would go through the answers together, and if there was something that was maybe a little bit off, I would point it out to her, like, "You know, this isn't good," or "You need to clarify this with him" ... I took her into the massage room, and I kind of just ran through how you give an erotic massage, and I told her if a guy books an hour, he wants a full hour. He doesn't want to finish after twenty minutes. I showed her how to do a body slide. I also told her how to be safe in terms of contracting STIs and whatnot.

Indeed, engaging in third party practices as a mechanism to provide assistance, while certainly contrary to the prevailing narrative of exploitation, is a recurring theme. Perhaps it is hardly surprising given the dynamics of the illicit industry. As we see throughout this collection, in the absence of the resources customarily available to workers (e.g., labour protection, established training protocols, occupational health-and-safety regulations) and to citizens (e.g., police protection, access to criminal-justice redress), participants in the sex industry turn to each other for support. Miss W. (outcall manager, Montreal) explained that barriers restricting access to conventional forms of criminal-justice protection "also puts a lot of pressure [on her]" because it means assuming "responsibility for their [sex workers'] safety, it really stresses me out." In short, in a criminalized context social and friendship networks take on the additional significance of a mechanism through which to mitigate workplace risks – risks that include criminalization. Star, a street-based peer facilitator who would book calls for sex workers and allow the women to use her room in supportive housing to see clients, was cognizant that she not only provided workers with a safer service-provision space but was also "help[ing] these girls to avoid our common enemy, which is the police."

The genesis of this desire to provide assistance varied. Ironically, given the prevailing trope of third parties as violent and exploitative men, Star suggested that this "care work"[8] was consistent with conventional gender roles: "If you're a girl who grows up in a culture where girls are supposed to provide and serve anyway ... the culture promotes women taking care of men. So I just broadened that to taking care of everybody." Some, like Rhonda, a workplace provider in Toronto, who appreciates (and struggles with) the class mobility afforded by the sex industry, are committed to "pay[ing] it forward." In rather striking contrast to the "pimp lobby" narrative discussed in the Foreword and Introduction, she unpacks how her commitment to social justice informs her third party work:

> Somebody took the risk for me for a long time – financial risk, legal risk. And now it's an opportunity for me – knowing more and being more experienced – to take that risk for somebody else and to share it with them. My political commitment to sex working communities informs a lot of what I do ... I really like the opportunity to be building a space that I can believe in, that fits with my values and my political vision of how women, in particular, should be able to work together.

The sense of community and collegiality noted by Rhonda is particularly significant in a clandestine industry – something that was highlighted by third parties who embrace this work as a mechanism through which to foster emotional well-being. At first Brenda (incall agency owner, Toronto), a thirty-seven-year-old mother of three who started working as an escort to pay off the debt incurred when her husband's business failed, "didn't know anybody in the industry ... there was really no support system." She met other sex workers through a mutual client and began sharing her incall space with one of them; she was delighted that "it just snowballed into this wonderful little adventure where I've got ten girls working with me on a regular basis." Similarly, Lilith (mentor, Ottawa) appreciated the "companionship" of working with another sex worker, while Lisa (incall agency owner, Toronto) highlighted the importance of collegiality in the context of social isolation engendered by stigma, explaining that "just to have some other women to share that with so that you don't feel so isolated, other women that understand, that are in the same position you are, that aren't going to stereotype. I liked that – the camaraderie."

While some sex workers who became third parties are determined to provide assistance, improve working conditions, establish good labour practices, create community, and ensure security, many are simultaneously motivated by potential earnings. Given the subsistence street economy, this meant Fanny, a peer facilitator in Ottawa, "was making a little bit of money. I was making a little bit of my drugs." Star explained "It was just my day-to-day survival and getting along, getting what I need and helping somebody out at the same time." By contrast, Punk (street-based agent, Halifax) saw third party work as a means through which to exit the sex industry:

> I was hanging out with prostitutes and smoking crack with them, and I thought, "If they can do it, I can do it." And so I started working the streets. And I hated it, absolutely hated it. But if it meant getting twenty dollars for a rock [of crack cocaine] then I was going to do it. And then I got thinking, "Well, I don't really have to do it if I can get somebody else to do it, then I can get a percentage of that." So it just started.

For some the road into management entails weighing the real and potential social and economic costs with the prospective financial and other, less tangible, benefits. Lisa (incall agency owner, Toronto), Carole (incall agency owner, Toronto), and Beatrice (outcall agency owner, Hamilton) purchased the agencies where they worked only after careful reflection on the significant investment of time and money and the potential risk of criminalization[9] and eviction. Other times, becoming a proprietor happens serendipitously. Stéphanie, who was working as an escort in Montreal, found herself the owner of an outcall agency after her friends began asking her to send them her surplus clients. Sandi (event planner, Montreal) was also working as an independent escort when "a client … contacted me and asked if I would come to a party but that I would need more people than just me." Dex (strip club manager, Toronto), who lost his job when the bar closed as the result of mismanagement, felt that "my only recourse at that period of time was to attempt to reopen it." Along with some members of the previous managerial team, Dex "built a business plan and reopened the business." Unlike many third parties who balance their responsibilities with sex work, Dex's adoption of this new role necessitated that he stop dancing – something he enjoyed – because, for him, "it's just unethical to be managing and then taking the money away from your employees."

Whichever pathway and motivation led them to establish or purchase commercial sex establishments, these sex workers turned third parties need to draw not only on their knowledge of the sex industry but also on the skills learned in other areas of their lives. For example, Beatrice, who had previously run a successful cleaning service, noted that her father "was an entrepreneur, I think that taught me a lot, just seeing how he had managed his companies." Others found that the skills they developed in mainstream labour sectors were transferable. Rhonda "worked as a research coordinator in an academic research centre and oversaw a number of research assistants. So assigning them tasks, making sure they came in on time, submitting their pay to payroll for them to get paid, checking their work, assigning them work, supervising, delegating, that kind of stuff." A few, like Carole, an incall agency owner in Toronto who already had "an honours diploma in business administration," had "no problems with math, bookkeeping, accounting, dealing with money" and so sought out additional training and went "back to college for writing so I can write better ads."

Not all sex workers turned third parties own and operate a business. As in any other service sector, there is a stratum of third parties who are middle managers, supervisors (e.g., receptionists, bookers), or service providers (e.g., drivers, security). Some third parties, like Marie (massage parlour manager, Montreal), proactively sought out third party opportunities. More often (middle) management was not so much a pursued goal as a seized opportunity. This was the case for Jackie, an outcall agency receptionist in Toronto:

> I was actually working for the agency as a worker, as one of the girls, and I had some health issues, I had to take some time off. That coincided with the time that the receptionist left. So I had kind of gotten close with my boss … and he said "Why don't you do it? You're good on the phone, you've worked reception before." I said, "Sure."

Similarly Miss W., a forty-year-old former erotic dancer and current escort, started her managerial career in a Montreal outcall agency when "the manager really took on a shine to my organizational skills." By contrast, Justine, a former phone-sex operator, was actively recruited when she was just out of high school:

> A woman who owned one of those phone sex companies called me and said, "I know someone who needs someone to answer the phones for an escort business ... you know, you're just what he needs." So, I said, "I'll try it out, sure." And she said, "He has the money and he has the girls to do this and he just needs someone good on the phone. And you will make this guy a million." I said, "Okay." And I did. I made the man very, very rich ... And I loved the business. I was on the phone. I was making already $1000 a week just answering phones. Yes, it went from a non-existent company to like the biggest company, to the biggest in the city.

While we hear pride, pleasure, and welcomed challenges in Justine's narrative, this is not a sentiment shared by all. There are sex workers who move into third party work not because it is a desirable option but rather due to a lack of alternatives. At times – and consistent with the classic "madam narrative" – an aging sex worker starts managing other workers when her (or his) income declines. For example, Leah, an Ottawa-area woman who describes herself as French-Aboriginal, became an incall/outcall agency manager when she was told she was too old to continue as an escort and "they put me in charge of booking appointments and stuff for other girls." A sex worker since the age of sixteen, Édouard (agent, Québec City) found that at forty-six his marketability in pornography was diminishing. He noted: "Before that I did lots of films in Los Angeles, I realized ... I couldn't make money anymore. So I decided to use my name in the prostitution business."[10] He eventually expanded his business by representing other sex workers.

Before leaving this section it should be noted that the transition into third party work is not always seamless. Like any worker moving into a supervisory role, it can necessitate grappling with changing relationships to erstwhile colleagues, negotiating roles and responsibilities, and adapting to shifting status markers. Rhonda (incall location provider, Toronto), who became "interested in management ... at the same time that I realized that it [sex work] was something I wanted to do longer term," enjoys providing workers with "access to a space that's safe and clean and good" but also struggles with the "power and privilege" of her position.

Sometimes It's Just About Who You Know

While many third parties are, or were, sex workers, others enter this work without previous experience in the sex industry. For many of these individuals in the incall, outcall, street, and (to a lesser extent) erotic dance sectors of the industry, opportunities emerge through their social, familiar, or mainstream work networks. Suzy got her receptionist job at a Toronto massage parlour through "one of the managers [who] also worked with these other guys who had a couple massage parlours" at the car dealership where she worked. She had let him know that she was "looking for a part-time job ... and he was like, 'Okay, well, why don't you come work reception there.' "

In other cases the entry of individuals who are already knowledge-able, or in Goffman's (1963) language "wise," about the sex industry is facilitated by their (semi) insider status and family connections. This was certainly the case for Robert, a street-based third party in Halifax who defined himself as a "caretaker" and whose job was to "watch [his girlfriend's] back." He noted "it's always good to have family that had the background. I learned a lot from my uncle. He's done the same type of thing." By contrast Joe, a fifty-one-year-old white man with three children and a current website provider in Toronto, became involved when:

> My wife answered an ad in the newspaper, thinking it was a receptionist job. And, after the interview, she realized that it was actual escorting. And she thought about it and gave it a try. And within a couple of months, we decided that we could do this on our own as far as operating an agency. So, we opened up our agency and were relatively successful for the next eighteen years.

Other times, knowing people in the sex industry puts an individual at the right place at the right time. For example George, who was offered a job as a strip club doorman, explained: "I dated an ex-dancer. I went to the club a few times, made friends with the other doormen. [I] just happened to go in there one day with a large group of people. And they needed a doorman. So I got the job." At other times, and evoking images of "drug dealer pimps" – at the same time as they challenge the script that frames all such relationships as exploitative – individuals who sell illicit substances became third parties.[11] Paul (Halifax) who "was a dope dealer" found "it all went hand in hand." Daddy (agent,

Toronto), a Black Torontonian who drew attention to the stereotypes when he remarked "I'm not a pimp but I play one on TV," explained that he had given little thought to becoming a third party:

> I started letting two girls stay with me – they were actually just out of jail … They had been dancing and escorting, and I hooked them up with a security guy I knew at a strip joint so they could dance. And through my work and being out with me on the hustle, guys would ask about them and I'd hook them up that way to do that work. They liked girls, so they used to bring other girls around, and after a couple of months it ended up that I was staying with the four of them and taking their [clients'] calls.

There are also situations were third party work is not so much facilitated by social or familial relations as defined (and confined) by these relationships. This was the case for John, an upper-middle-class white man who was "friends with benefits" with a woman he met in the military. When she started escorting he became her driver simply "because she asked me." Vanessa's (outcall agency owner, Montreal) sex work and her work as a third party came about through an intimate relationship as well: "My partner was a voyeur. And I was going with men for free. We asked ourselves, 'Why not do this for money?' … I started working [as an escort] alone. After that I added workers."[12]

Advertisements in the Classifieds

So far we have seen that the pathways into third party work echo those taken by workers in other jobs – experience in the industry or "knowing people." Nowhere is this more evident than when third parties enter the strip and incall/outcall sex industry in the most banal of ways – through the classifieds. Fuzzy (DJ, Ottawa) was nineteen, unemployed, and staying with family when his "uncle looked in the newspaper and said, 'Hey, they're looking for a DJ at the Starfish,' which is a strip club, so I went down. I said, 'Hey, I'm here to apply for the DJ job.' They put me on the mic and they hired me. That was it." Guy and Sam, both from Québec City, were unemployed when they answered advertisements in the newspaper to become drivers. Kaya (outcall agency receptionist, Toronto), who had previously worked as a phone-sex operator, "called the number that was given [in the classifieds]. It was just kind of like, 'hello' – very sexy, sensuous. So I knew right away I wasn't going to like an insurance company's organization."

Just like any other labour sector, individuals in the sex industry sometimes parlay these advertised entry-level jobs into other
positions – climbing the "corporate ladder" and taking on additional
responsibilities in the process. For example, Adam (strip club manager,
Toronto) started as a bouncer before working as a DJ and finally a manager, assuming ever-greater administrative duties. Troy's (strip club DJ,
Toronto) trajectory was unintentional: "My background is radio. So I've
always been a DJ ... One day the manager didn't show up so I did the
managerial duties that day and DJ'd and they thought that was great.
Why would I hire two people when one person can do two jobs? So
that's [laughter] followed me ever since."

Accidental "Pimps"[13]

The last pathway category is the most unexpected, and it is certainly
inconsistent with the "pimp" mythology. At the same time it does not
reflect mainstream labour-market trajectories either. Two of the third
parties were accidental "pimps." Eric (protection/driver, Toronto) was
approached by an erotic dancer who asked him to drive and "look out for
her." Bee (street third party, Toronto) explains that his involvement "was
just circumstances, things happen": he found himself with the identity of
street-based "pimp" (providing protection) thrust upon him. He was a
lonely fifteen-year-old living on the streets of Toronto when a twenty-year-
old woman who he "didn't really know was a hooker" befriended him:

> I was just this homeless, wandering, upset, lost young guy, and then every
> night I would just kind of go around there because she would tell me,
> "Okay, come back tomorrow. I'll see you tomorrow. We'll talk more; we'll
> chill." And she'd buy me sodas and shit, always giving me, like, five or ten
> bucks before she left at, like, three, four in the morning.

When his newfound friend realized Bee was homeless, "she took
me to her apartment. And then, basically, I just started staying there
every night. And I would just leave in the daytime, do my own thing,
meet her at night." He describes (unknowingly) providing security: "I
would just sit there, in the background, and no one would bug her.
And I started realizing that by me being around her she felt more
safe." At this time, Bee explained, while "I cared about her as a friend,
I wasn't making any money, and I didn't care. I was just happy to have
a friend." However his (private) self-identity was at odds with how he

was being "read" – his public identity (Goffman, 1956). He explained that "all these other pimps started coming around and talking to me ... They thought I was lying to them. They thought I was this little, young pimp, right, and I was pimping this girl." Ultimately, in part seduced by the friendship and sense of belonging offered by these men, Bee did come to play a more active third party role on the street (although never in relation to the woman who inadvertently "turned him out"). He reflected that he "didn't know anything ... My dad was abusive, like beyond belief – physically, mentally, emotionally. So to me, I was just happy to be accepted and be making fucking money."

Challenges, Conundrums, and the "Good Stuff"

Bee's story alerts us to some of the challenges of being a third party and the complexity of identity (see also Hannem and Bruckert, 2016). It is hardly surprising that third parties find navigating identity challenging. After all they are well aware that public opinion defines them as "a user ... one of the bad guys taking advantage of some poor soul's circumstances" (Fanny, peer facilitator, Ottawa). As a result many third parties, drawing on a classic stigma management strategy, endeavour to "pass" (Goffman, 1963) by hiding their (deviant) labour identity: "when you talk to the general public, you have to pretend you don't do what you do. I always just say that I'm a student and I have no money because you don't want to go into the whole explanation of why you're in the industry that you're in" (Brittany, incall/outcall agency owner, Ottawa). This strategy, of course, denies individuals the ability to "share [their] success with people" (Sophie, incall/outcall agency owner, Ottawa). It also necessitates creating a cover story when dealing with financial and other professionals: "I had to make up business cards of a fictitious business in the beginning and pretend that I'm doing something else" (Joe, owner-operator outcall agency, Toronto).

While social judgment and the need to negotiate public identity was identified as a negative aspect of the work for many third parties, "passing" is easier for those who do not conform to gendered and racialized stereotypes. This not only simplifies social interactions but also, as Lisa (incall agency owner, Toronto) points out, decreases the risk of being criminalized:

I don't look like whatever the stereotypical image is, right ... there's a lot of privilege that comes with that and I'm very aware of that and I don't take that for granted ... [But] if being a white woman of a certain look and of a certain education level, that sort of thing, helps me manoeuvre some of these hurdles and some of these legal ramifications better – then that's what I have to do in order to protect myself.

Indeed criminalization was a particular concern for racialized men like Robert (street manager, Halifax), who told us: "They'd rather have you in jail if you're a Native than have you on the street." For Daddy, a "Trini-flavoured" Toronto-based agent, "the police angle, you know, you're always worried, you can't sleep too heavy." Others, particularly mothers like Justine, worried not only about criminal charges but also about losing custody of their children.

Other challenges were more banal, echoing those experienced by third parties of mainstream service-provision businesses: "It's like with every business, it's not just this industry that there's fucked up people, or normal people, or challenges in the day-to-day operation – it's just life" (EJ, massage parlour owner, Toronto). Specific challenges are of course determined by a range of factors, including industry sector, nature of the third party's responsibilities/roles, social location (which conditions options at one's disposal), professional and personal strengths and weaknesses, and personality. A number of third parties noted that dealing with clients can be frustrating: "You have a lot of nasty people call in. People who make you waste your time. And the perverts. And people who are not very friendly or people that make an appointment but ultimately do not show up"[14] (Luna, incall manager, Montreal). Others spoke of the "drama" and complained about worker unreliability (see also Chapter 4, this collection). Unpredictability came up in various other ways as well: "It's basically, like, a fourteen-hour-a-day, seven-day-a-week job" (Lilith, mentor, Ottawa), and therefore can, as Sandi, an event planner in Montreal, pointed out, "have a significant impact and disruption in my personal life." Since most third parties are paid a percentage or flat rate per service, rather than a wage, income can be unstable and "you can't plan how much money you're going to make because you don't know from one day to the next" (Pierrette, personal assistant, Ottawa). This is particularly hard for owners and managers of agencies who have to balance ensuring adequate staff to meet client demand with the need for workers to earn money (while remaining mindful that workers will find other third party arrangements should income prove inadequate). Middle managers (which in the sex industry would include receptionists, DJs, and bookers), as in other labour market sectors, struggle with a contradictory labour location (Willmott, 1997). In some cases they are imposing rules on the same sex workers they rely upon for their direct or indirect ("tip") income (Law, this collection); they are required to enforce rules (which they may or may not feel are fair) without a great deal of authority to, for example, discipline or terminate workers:

> [Sex workers] give me a hard time about dressing. It's a requirement that the customer wants, it's not a requirement that I want. So I'm just doing what I'm asked to do. But then there's … an hour of arguing and negotiating, and finally they give in to me and say, "Fine I'll do it." But it's not for me – I'm not gaining anything out of this. (Leah, incall/outcall manager, Toronto)

Resentment toward management and a perception (whether accurate or not) that they are disproportionately compensated for their contribution is no doubt a sentiment shared widely among Canadian workers. In the sex industry this is layered over the pervasive "exploitative pimp" trope. Perhaps unsurprisingly given that sex workers, too, are social actors, they sometimes "buy into" the stereotypes, and while they desire third party services, they are also resentful that individuals "get a cut out of their work" (Kaya, outcall agency receptionist, Toronto). Bridgette, an incall/outcall agency manager in Ottawa, explained her strategy to manage this intra-industry stigma: "Sometimes they see you as just there to take their money, like they don't realize you do work as hard as they do … I like the girls to see me working. I like them to see me booking calls. I like them to see me planning the advertising. I like them to see me doing anything involved in management."

In spite of the challenges of the job, social judgment, and criminalization, third parties also report that they enjoy their work. Indeed many relish the same things sex workers do – the freedom, the autonomy, and the chance to meet people who, in the normal course of events, they would be unlikely to encounter.[15] Carole, a Toronto incall agency owner, explained that she also appreciates "being my own boss. I like the relationships with the girls. I like knowing I'm making a difference." Others like the excitement, the variety, and the "edginess": "I felt like I had a secret cool life where I made money … I was working with the hoes, you know what I mean? Like, I was doing this kind of work that was not even thought of or considered in my circle of work colleagues [at her other job]" (Kaya, outcall receptionist, Toronto).

For some, however, the reward of the job is "mostly financial … a means to an end" (Chico, DJ, Ottawa). Like many other workers who labour for economic security, the importance of monetary benefit does not preclude other aspects of the work being positive and affirming. Chico went on to explain, for example, that at times his job is validating: "On a good night, when you've got the right audience and you've got a couple of funny lines that come out of you and the whole crowd laughs and the girls laugh and everybody enjoys it and when you walk out of the bar, that's like being on stage, you know? It's like I just sang three songs, and the crowd gave me a standing ovation." Finally, and circling back to the beginning of the chapter, a significant number of third parties appreciated that they were "helping out" (Brenda, incall agency owner, Toronto) by, for example, "bring[ing] stability into their [sex workers] lives" (Daddy, agent, Toronto). Horeta (incall agency manager, Halifax), who "felt good" about "providing a safe work environment," even found herself operating against her own financial interests: "I've … had girls that came and worked for me, and I told them, 'Honey, you know you need to get another job. You're not made for this. Someone's going to kill you.' "

Pathways Out: Leaving Third Party Work

Just like there are a variety of pathways to becoming a third party, the thirty-three participants who had relinquished this role did so for a wide range of reasons. Some of these reasons echo those of workers in mainstream sectors – disagreements with bosses, the emergence of new opportunities, or waning interest. Beyond these, participants shared a range of other factors that pushed them out of the sex industry. For example Mercedes (receptionist, incall agency, Toronto) and Brad (security, Toronto) quit the sex industry when they stopped consuming illicit substances. For Punk (street-based agent, Halifax) it was likewise part of a larger lifestyle change; she explained that she "got tired of it. I wanted to stay off, get off the drugs and get away from the whole situation, and that's what I've done." Bee, who started to "feel guilty" after reading the Bible and Qu'ran in jail, cut all ties with the sex industry.

In many cases personal circumstances and shifting priorities motivated the change of employment. For example when Trixie (outcall agency owner, Toronto) got pregnant she left the industry, whereas Adèle (owner-operator outcall agency, Montreal) sold her agency in order to make time for herself. Similarly Ava (Ottawa), Leah (Toronto), and Coco (Montreal), all of whom were incall/outcall managers, had trouble balancing their managerial responsibilities with their personal lives. In striking contradiction to the narrative that third parties make easy money, Leah explained that it was "too much work, not enough time for myself, so I was starting to stress out and ... I have kids and my kids will come first." Similarly Miss W. (outcall agency owner, Montreal) found "it's so stressful being on call for eighteen hours a day" and concluded that "it's not worth it. I'll be poor instead."

Other third parties left their managerial roles behind because they conflicted with, or caused conflicts in, their intimate relationships. For example Daddy (agent, Toronto) phased out of management when "I got serious with my girl. I wanted to do something more. I stopped going out and being out in the late-night scene all the time, which shut down a lot of availability and opportunities that came up." The same was true for Stephanie (outcall agency owner, Québec City). By contrast, John (driver, Ottawa) ceased being a third party when his relationship with the friend he drove deteriorated and Vicky's role as a third party organizing bookings and ensuring security for herself and her partner in Toronto ended along with this romantic relationship.

Just as some individuals draw on their experience in sex work to become third parties, others use their experience in the sex industry to transition into mainstream jobs. Scott (Ottawa) started working security in a strip club as a student summer job: "I figured, why not have a little fun, you know? Bounce a little. I heard that it was, uh, an entertaining job." Having profited from the experience and professional contacts he cultivated during this period, he now runs his own security company: "While bouncing at the first exotic dance club, I made connections and I started getting a variety of security work outside. I started doing concerts, I started doing private parties. I learned a lot because of the connections I made. I found that a lot of it related to why I got the work that I got today."

Not everyone who transitioned out of third party work did so by choice. Suzy (incall/outcall receptionist) "was fired." Ten other participants (seven indoor third parties and three who worked in the street-based industry) had few options but to turn to another line of work after being criminally convicted for their activities as third parties. Some, like Joe, transitioned into different kinds of third party work in the sex industry, while others moved into mainstream labour sectors. Fanny (peer facilitator, Ottawa) spoke of using her arrest to transform her life: "When they let me out on bail, I asked them to remand me to a [different] shelter, not back to [shelter name]. I abandoned everything I owned." She explained that she "thought, you know what? If I go back, I'm never going to get out of this whirlpool."

Tandy's (incall agency manager, Ottawa) somewhat different trajectory certainly serves as a cautionary tale. The collective brothel she managed came to the attention of law enforcement when "one guy didn't feel fully satisfied when the time was up, so he went right down the street and told the police." Tandy "took the rap for everything, I pled guilty to it all. Because they [the other women involved in the business] had kids and stuff, I wasn't going to let them lose their kids." As a result she had to pay fines and do "a little bit of jail time." More to the point, with a criminal record for prostitution charges her options both in and out of the sex industry are limited. Tandy explains how this resonates in her life years later:

> The business closed, [which] brought me back to the street … I ended up becoming a major drug addict, you know. It was my first family and we were happy … [The arrest] didn't just wreck the business, it wrecked the atmosphere, it wrecked the family, it wrecked closeness. It wrecked a lot of things.

Concluding Reflections

This chapter fleshed out who third parties are by drawing from the narratives of participants in the Management Project and their accounts of why and how they came to be third parties, as well as why some left these positions. Here we see factors such as entrepreneurialism, career development, personal networks and contacts, circumstance, opportunity, serendipity, financial need, interest, and relationships. Many, but self-evidently not all, of these factors mirror mainstream career paths. After all it is not uncommon for waitresses to become shift supervisors and line workers to become forepersons. Nor is it unusual for particularly entrepreneurial individuals to learn about a business and then, after careful consideration of the costs (including the time and energy required to build and maintain a business) and the benefits (such as autonomy and potential earnings), to "strike out on their own." Of course risks enter into the equation as well – but here we come back to the specificity of the sex industry: unlike mainstream businesses, sex industry third parties are stigmatized and criminalized. In real terms this means they risk not only financial loss (as does anybody who starts a business) but also their reputation, social status, and indeed their liberty.

Notes

1 Sixty-three per cent of our sample was composed of women.
2 The 2016 analysis of the 2014 data found that 4 per cent of Canadians reported physical or sexual abuse in an intimate relationship in the past five years. 10 per cent reported emotional and/or financial abuse.
3 For more on the range of relationships, see Bruckert and Law, 2013.
4 See Introduction (this collection) for methodology.
5 See Introduction (this collection) for an overview of the methodological approach of the project.
6 Fourteen individuals did not identify their ethnicity.
7 Some agencies fine sex workers for infractions such as being late or the failure to work a shift for which they were scheduled.
8 This links to Megan Rivers-Moore's (2016) work on the Costa Rican sex industry, in which she examines sex work as care work.
9 Most explicitly under the "procuring" (CC s. 236.3) and "materially benefiting" from another's sexual service provisions (CC s. 286.2).
10 Translated passage.
11 This was the situation for two third parties who participated in the research.
12 Translated passage.
13 The term *pimp* is being used ironically here. The individuals meet the legal criteria of procurers and their roles conform to the stereotype – even if their methods do not.
14 Translated passage.
15 See for example Jeffrey and MacDonald, 2006.

3 Through the Voices of Female Sex Workers: The Street Managers

PATRICE CORRIVEAU AND COLETTE PARENT

Many scholars have examined the question of sex work and female sex workers in diverse workplaces, but, as we see throughout this collection, few have taken an interest in the question of managers on the street. Street-based managers are defined in this chapter as individuals who organize, supervise, and/or coordinate the work of one or several sex workers (usually women) who solicit clients on the street. These individuals, normatively referred to as "pimps," have come to symbolize the professional manipulator, the exploiter, even the violent parasite. Studies conducted on the experience of particular subsamples of female sex workers and from the viewpoint of police have helped to reinforce this image. However, there is little research based on the voices of these street "pimps" themselves. The Management Project conducted interviews with nine street-based third parties whose experiences are presented in Chapter 2: "Who Are Third Parties?" In this chapter we foreground the data collected in a series of focus-group interviews with female sex workers, and it is from the discourse of female sex workers that we trouble the portrayals of street-based "pimps." Before discussing our empirical findings, we survey the scholarly literature to unpack the stereotype of the "pimp" and examine the portraits that emerge from the limited empirical research in which we hear from these individuals themselves.

The "Pimp": A Threat to Public Morality?

Looking at the figure of the "pimp" historically, we can observe that his social representation has been quite consistent throughout the centuries.[1] In medieval times, jurists of canon law considered the "pimp" the most despicable participant in the sex industry. For instance, although sex work was defined as immoral, only "pimps" were criminally targeted. In London, the sentence for "pimping" was the pillory for the first offence, the pillory and ten days in prison for the second offence, and expulsion from the city for the third offence (Gleeson, 2004). The church held that "pimping" encouraged debauchery and threatened the spiritual life of Christians, and that it therefore had to be repressed.

Even in the twentieth century procuring was the target of generalized social reprobation. "Pimps" were blamed, for example, for appropriating most, if not all, of the worker's earnings without having done any work at all. Whether or not it is a fair analysis, Gleeson (2004) notes that this type of labour relation – which appears to be based on the exploitation of one of the parties involved – could describe various types of jobs, not just sex work. Moreover, she observes, that "pimps" may play a significant role in protecting workers from the police and from violence. Why, then, is the "pimp" hated so much?

To answer this question, Gleeson examines the production of law in English and Australian jurisdictions. She looks, more specifically, at two important steps in the regulation of prostitution in both countries: (1) the enactment of the "common prostitute" statute at the beginning of the nineteenth century, and (2) the Wolfenden Report published in 1957. She thus covers the parliamentary debates on prostitution in both countries during this period. Her data shows that prostitution is (re)defined as the result of a "natural human need" and not "free choice." The client is seen as a feeble man responding to his physiological needs, while the "pimp" is an abusive individual taking advantage of the "natural" human weakness of others. Moreover, in doing so, the "pimp" shows that prostitution is not natural – that it is not a response to the needs of men by available women who, by nature, lack will-power, modesty, and are sexual. In fact, the "pimp" demonstrates that prostitution is a business run for profit.

The laws adopted during these periods targeted the "pimps" and not the clients (i.e., they took into consideration the exploitation of the clients by "pimps" but did not refer to the exchange between prostitutes and clients). For legislators, the "pimp," who profits from these transactions and whose presence questions the conception of prostitution as a necessary evil, was a threat first and foremost to men.

Literature Review

Although there is much academic literature on sex work and female sex workers, the same cannot be said of the management of sex work, including those who operate on the street – the figure that is most frequently evoked. Indeed, research and analysis has been slowly rolling out since the nineteenth century. In the following section we present diverse portraits of "pimps," most of them involving an approach that highlights his fundamental difference from other human beings – a negative difference, it goes without saying. Some of these portraits feed on conventional or feminist moral indignation; others are based on relatively carefully collated psychological or sociological data. There are also analyses that shift attention away from the "pimp" and seek instead to shed light on the organization of sex work, positioning the "pimp" as a member of this institution. This research may be contrasted with studies based specifically on interviews with female sex workers that adopt the approach that she either works with, or is exploited by, a "pimp." Finally, several studies have managed to take as their point of departure the voice of *street* "pimps." This rather sparse research allows for a unique understanding of the figure of the "pimp" and presents the organization of "pimping" as a form of service.

The "Pimp": A Monster

In some studies, the "pimp" is described as the very personification of evil. The work of Mancini (1972) and, especially, Chaleil (1981) are classic examples of this. These studies, based on existing texts – testimonials by judges, police officers, physicians, writers, "pimps," sex workers, and others – take the form of essayistic reflections rather than scientific research. In short, this body of literature focuses more on denunciation than careful observation. The resulting portrait of the "pimp" is an unambiguous condemnation: "These 'human worms,' these leeches that sponge off the prostitute and feed on her very substance" (Chaleil, 1981, 355, our translation). Craven, weak, cruel, and utterly pitiless (Mancini, 1972), they lead women into prostitution using persuasion, collusion, trickery, love and seduction, blackmail, rape, hitting, mistreatment, torture, isolation, threats to their children, kidnapping, and the threat of deportation (Chaleil, 1981). Cut off from their past, these victims lose all autonomy, and even their identities.

This portrait was revived in the 1990s by neo-prohibitionist propo-
nents of Chaleil's (1981) thesis that "prostitution and trafficking go
together and [that] it is artificial to separate them, as the lines here are so
vague" (363, our translation). In this context, they denounce the "pimp"
as the embodiment of a system of domination that "legitimizes, legal-
izes, and organizes politically, economically, symbolically, culturally,
and doctrinally … the sex trade, the market in people" (Louis, 2006,
n.p., our translation). It would thus be related to slavery and colonial-
ism. In this view, the "pimp" is the keystone of the evil organization (see
also Barry, 1995; Poulin, 2004).

The "Pimp": A Different Character

Some analyses, in the wake of the traditional criminological approach
to prostitution, regard the "pimp" as fundamentally different from
other people and as primarily responsible for the "social problem" of
prostitution. These authors do not focus on biological differences, as do
studies on sex workers; rather, they observe psychological problems or
forms of social organization that lead individuals to become "pimps."
It must also be noted that, in contrast to traditional analyses of prostitutes – which generally ignore customers and managers – research
focusing on "pimps" includes observations of the relationship between
these various social actors.

Studies on "pimps" that seek to discern a psychological basis for their
difference invoke neurosis or psychopathy. In the few psychoanalytic
works published on the subject in the mid-twentieth century, "pimping" and neurosis are linked (Choisy, 1961; Greenwald, 1958; Winick and
Kinsie, 1971). In this view, the "pimp" might be, for example, an impo-
tent individual who prefers fellatio to other forms of sexual relations; he
might manifest latent homosexual tendencies and derive homosexual
pleasure from sharing "his woman" with other men; or he might deny
his homosexuality and enter into competition with the customers. A few
psychoanalysts have also analysed the relationships between prostitutes
and "pimps." They diagnose "pimps" as suffering from complementary
neurosis and developing a degrading, sadomasochist dynamic with
female sex workers. What is more, since neither the "pimp" nor the sex
worker is capable of developing intimate connections, this shared inability attracts them to each other and helps to cement their relationship.

In the twenty-first century, Spidel et al. (2006) expressed surprise that
so little research had been done on the "pimp" as psychopath. After

presenting connections between the characteristics of "pimps" identified in the literature and psychopathic traits, these scholars developed a research protocol to evaluate prisoners on a psychopathy scale. They selected a sample of twenty-two men detained (in three correctional institutions in British Columbia) for procuring/living on the avails of prostitution (at that time this was contrary to s. 212 of the *Criminal Code*), and whose files contained a score in the Psychopathy Checklist – Revised (PCL-R). People trained to administer the PCL-R conducted semi-directed interviews with these prisoners and analysed them according to the checklist's criteria and the data recorded in their respective files. The results indicate that people imprisoned for having lived off the proceeds of prostitution obtained a higher psychopathy score than did a control group of 5,408 North American adult male correctional inmates and also scored higher on certain interpersonal and affective variables (crafty, manipulative, hard, indifferent). These results, even though based on a very limited sample and without any control group, suggested to the authors that a large number of female sex workers are likely to enter into contact with a psychopathic "pimp" and, as a corollary, suffer emotionally and physically. The authors conclude that these findings should be taken into account by politicians when considering health and/or criminal justice policies.[2]

The "Pimp" Defined by His Social Role

Other authors have looked at the "pimp's" social integration. In 1931, Reitman proposed a functionalist analysis of the phenomenon. He examined the individual traits, motivations, and behaviours of the "pimps" he interviewed while he was himself serving a prison sentence. Reitman found that the "pimp" fulfils a number of functions. First, he protects the sex worker from criminal intervention by buying police inaction or paying fines. He plays the role of placement officer by choosing the bordellos or the section of the city where street-based sex work is tolerated. He protects the worker from customers or (other) third parties who might be violent towards her. He also plays the role of mentor by teaching her about the business, supervising her consumption of drugs and alcohol, handling suicide attempts, and/or controlling her through expressions of affection or anger. Reitman also estimated that most "pimps" are violent towards their women: according to him, some use violence only when they have a "reasonable excuse"; others, too cowardly to take on a man, hit their women to blow off steam when they are unhappy with a situation.

It should be noted that Reitman examined "pimping" in terms of the relationship between "pimp" and worker, even though his work drew solely on interviews conducted with incarcerated procurers. He presented sex workers as immoral women predisposed to prostitution due to biological determinants or mental deficiencies. In his view, fear and submission originate in the psychic or hypnotic power that the "pimp" exerts over an already consenting woman.

The ethnographic work of Milner and Milner (1972) introduces us to the African American subculture of the street "pimp": "players" who (in the community they researched) control the prostitution market and female sex workers (referred to as "hos") organized in "families" under the infallible authority of the "pimp," who may resort to violence. In these families, social relationships between men and women are strongly polarized: sex workers offer their services to customers and bring the revenue back to the house, while the "pimps" ostentatiously display their wealth and status and socialize with friends in bars. According to Milner and Milner, these men assert that male-female relations are based on sexual roles dictated by nature. This natural hierarchy must be respected if society is to function properly. The authors suggest that the "pimp" or player who presents himself as a god to his women is also seen in the Black community as having overcome white peoples' traditional domination over African American slaves in the United States. He dominates white and Black women, profits financially from the white customers whose money he takes, and challenges the conventional racial tropes by subjecting white sex workers to his authority (Milner and Milner, 1972, 216). If he has an agenda, its main tenant is an individual revolution in a community dominated by whites. Given this logic, it is perhaps not surprising that some female African American sex workers who work with a "pimp" consider white men to be the enemy.

Other empirical studies target the figure of the street "pimp." These researches, based mainly on interviews with female sex workers, and sometimes with law enforcement, do not adopt an ethnographic approach. Whereas some authors examine street-based sex work activities as a whole and the social actors involved, including the "pimp," others emphasize the different forms of recruitment employed by "pimps" to convince women to work for them and ultimately to submit to their authority.[3] Finally, a number of researchers focus on the specific forms of violence of which sex workers may be the targets, including those perpetrated by the "pimp."[4] Overall, this research is in keeping with a representation of the relationship between "pimps" and street-based sex workers as one marked by exploitation and violence.

Criminalization of the "Pimp" and the Impact on Sex Workers

In addition to the above-noted research, which reinforces the portrayal of the "pimp" as different (either psychologically or on the basis of subculture) and which describes "pimp"-worker relations as founded on exploitation and violence, there are studies that, consistent with the position outlined in Chapter 2 of this collection ("Who are Third Parties?"), frame the activities of these social actors as a form of work characterized by power relations that may or may not include control based on violence. These studies draw on interviews with female sex workers to examine how the criminalization of management activities has impacted their work and private lives (Currie and Gillies, 2006; van der Meulen, 2010). The findings suggest that criminal laws, far from protecting workers against exploitation by "pimps," increase their vulnerability to workplace risks and have a very negative effect on their private life, notably by reducing their partner to the role of violent exploiter. This research brings to light the state's responsibility with regard to the safety of sex workers because the law defines anyone who is habitually in the company of a sex worker as a "pimp" – someone who is essentially deviant and toxic to the workers.

The "Pimps" in Their Own View and That of the Workers

Finally, some studies are based on interviews with people whom the researchers define as "pimps." In this type of research the investigators generally have difficulty contacting participants. Only one study, conducted by May, Harocopos, and Hough (2006) for the Home Office in the United Kingdom, is based on a significant sample of managers of street-based sex work: individuals who, given their activities, could face charges related to living on the proceeds of prostitution (in Canada this is the "receiving a material benefit" provision contrary to s. 286.2 of the *Criminal Code*). Following the interviews, the authors divided their sample of 30 men into two categories: "classic pimps," who work on the street and, by their own admission, keep workers under constraint (15 individuals), and "partner pimps," men who do not identify themselves as "pimps" because they are associated with a single worker (15 individuals). The latter were, however, well aware that they could nevertheless be arrested and criminally charged.

Classic "pimps" acknowledged that they have a great deal of power over workers and admitted that they regulate almost all aspects of their lives. Only 4 of them indicated that they allow their workers to choose where they work. Three of these individuals pointed out that they provide "their women" with easy access to drugs. Most of them – 12 – felt that the workers receive benefits from their work alliance through the credibility that it gives them on the street and/or the protection that they receive. Interestingly, in the same research, interviews conducted with 19 women working with these individuals challenged the assertions that inform these interviews with the "pimps" – only one-third of the women stated that they draw benefits from their alliance with "pimps."

The 15 partner "pimps" in the May, Harocopos, and Hough (2006) study had a different profile in many ways. They offer much more support to the sex worker, and more than half stated that they "keep an eye on her" as she works. For instance, they may note the licence plate number of a customer's car and/or ensure that the worker can be contacted by cell phone. More than three-quarters of them were convinced that their partner is safer when they are close to the site of work, and only one stated that he chooses the work location on the street. Although a majority of them – 8 – believed that a manager protects the worker, 4 stated that they draw no advantage from the arrangement.

What conclusions can we draw from this scholarly literature? On the one hand, as we saw in the media analysis in Chapter 1 ("The Representation of the 'Pimp' "), the social view of the "pimp" is generally reduced to the figure of the exploiter, a vile and violent character. On the other hand, much of the research conducted from first-hand testimonials offers a more varied portrait of the labour and intimate relations between street managers and sex workers. We now turn to our own research.

The Street-Based Managers and the Work of Female Sex Workers

In this chapter we are interested in the relationships and behaviour of individuals who conform to the classic "pimp" definition – a street manager who supervises, controls, and/or coordinates the labour of street-based sex workers. Taking into account the limited number of interviews with third parties on the street (12), including managers and peer facilitators, and the symbolic importance of the role of the street "pimp," we turned to the data collected via focus-group interviews with sex workers in Ottawa, Toronto, and Halifax. A total of 17 street-based sex workers who had worked for a manager took part in this phase. The

focus-group interview protocol was formulated from individual interviews conducted previously with managers; it included questions
regarding the workers' health and safety, daily work activities, business ties to the manager, and personal relations between the two parties.[5] This process enabled us to grasp the importance of the place of
work – the street – as well as numerous aspects of the organization of
labour and labour relations from the perspectives of workers. It also
highlighted the diversity of relations between workers, managers, and
partners, and the ability of sex workers to position themselves as actors
responsible for their lives in a range of complex, and sometimes dangerous, situations.

Recruitment and Work Activities

The literature on "pimping" often talks about the recruitment of female
sex workers and, more precisely, the procedures used to trick young
women and draw them slowly into prostitution. In our individual interviews with managers of various types of sex work, we asked them if
they recruited workers. They indicated that, in fact, the workers chose
them: women on the street meet and talk with each other and recruitment occurs by word of mouth. Our focus-group interviews enabled
us to gather more details on the ways sex workers came to work for or
with a particular manager.

Chelsea told us that she met her manager when she was working
in a dance bar; he gave her his card and proposed that they meet to
discuss business. Lexus, a trans women, reported that it was a woman
who contacted her and invited her to her home: "She taught me how to
survive on the street" she recalled, "I'd be dead if not for her." Candy
remembered very well the circumstances under which she met the
individual she defined as her "man." At that time, she was "hanging
out" with drug buyers and sellers who met in a certain dwelling. One
night armed intruders entered and robbed everyone before returning
to burn down the house. Candy took refuge in an abandoned building where she met an individual with whom she began to spend time.
Already working as an independent sex worker, she started to work
for him. Despite the context of violence, Candy viewed this episode –
which she calls her "little love story" – positively. Wendy, on the other
hand, was introduced to sex work by a man she met on the street; he
offered her drugs to consume in his company. When she found herself
indebted to him, he pointed out a street where she could solicit clients
to earn money. That is how she began street-based sex work.

With regard to the sharing of daily tasks, the workers offer direct services to customers and the manager supervises these activities. There are no obvious rules with regard to the scheduling of work: sometimes it is the manager's responsibility; sometimes the worker simply informs him. Candy told us, for example, "I choose the right times, when there are customers, between one thirty and three o'clock." She is therefore assured of a good income and minimizes her time standing in a public place when there are no or few customers.

The managers we interviewed told us that they offer a variety of services, depending on the particular situation and relationship (e.g., protection, transportation, hotel rooms, customers); some supply food, makeup, clothing, and/or drugs. When we questioned the workers, a number, including Lily, who defines herself as an independent worker, stated that these individuals only offer protection services; otherwise she is independent. Others, such as Chelsea, noted that the arrangements vary by street: "On the high track all the girls have pimps and everything is organized for them – housing, food, shoes, clothing." On other streets, the arrangement varies according to the type of relationship between the manager and worker. Chelsea explained that "It depends on your other half ... Does he want to be your partner or simply set up a risk-free business?" The arrangement is also influenced by the woman involved, whether she wants everything supplied or just certain products or services that she cannot easily obtain (such as drugs that some customers request, or alcohol after hours). For instance, Chelsea likes to have a companion but she does not wish him to micromanage her affairs or dictate her work schedule. By contrast, Wendy explains, "He would walk down the street a little bit away from me, and he came mostly because I was new ... He would watch as I got into a car, and he would tell me to come back to the same spot. And if I was longer than, you know, half an hour, forty minutes, then – then he would start to worry, you know?" This individual also walked on the street a few steps away from her in order, he said, to protect her from other workers who might be irritated at her presence. He also let her stay in his apartment, supplied her with drugs, and offered her a safe consumption site.

Street-based managers do appear to impose certain work rules. When interviewed, they indicated that they require the workers to be professional: they must inform the customer of the services offered and the services excluded, provide good service, and not steal from clients. Yet this description raised incredulity among the workers who took part in the group interviews. They saw it as too idealistic a portrait, at least for managers on the street.

The managers we met also asserted that, if necessary, they physically threaten customers to ensure the worker is paid. By contrast, the sex workers stated that since they ask the customer for monetary compensation before they provide the service it is they, and not the manager, who must ensure payment. Lexus explains: "Like, I've had to extort guys so many times because you get in the car, and they're like, 'I changed my mind.' I'm like … 'you pulled over to me, wasted my time. You're giving me something for my time.' " Rianne specified that if the customer does not want to wear a condom, there is no agreement. Chelsea summarized the situation by stating that the workers are independent, unless an incident arises. In this respect, a situation reported by Rianne is enlightening. A regular customer paid her as usual at the beginning of the transaction, received the service requested, then stated "that it wasn't enough for him." He pointed a gun at her and took back the money he had paid, as well as all the money she had on her. After that, he pushed her out of the moving car. Rianne called her manager, who went looking for the pseudo-customer and found him on the street looking for drugs: "The guy," she said, "went away with no money and no self-esteem."

The managers we spoke with acknowledged that they expect a certain daily income. For their part, the workers noted that remitting a share is often a rule: although some are not expected to hand a percentage of their earnings to their manager on a daily basis, many others are required to do so. The profits generated by the work are shared in widely varying proportions. In the interviews, some managers indicated that they want 50 per cent, while others demanded 25 per cent or admitted that they ask for all the money but cover all expenses. Interviews with the workers confirmed that the distribution of money is highly variable. Lily hands over 80 per cent of her income to ensure her protection; Rianne pays 50 per cent to her partner, and whenever she asks a (contract) third party to keep an eye on the car she is getting into, she pays him ten dollars. In turn, she expects any partner-manager to divide his work profits with her as well. Candy pays everything to the manager she works for but feels that this protects her from her tendency to overspend: he gives her money when she asks. Rianne and Carissa hand over 30 per cent of their earnings to their female manager.

In interviews, the managers also mentioned several ways in which they penalize workers who do not follow the rules. Some managers verbally reprimand workers, use physical violence, and/or exclude them from social activities. The workers interviewed indicated that, if they do not bring in enough money, the consequences vary: some managers refuse to give them their share, leave them out of the "fun," or ignore them. Others demand they work to earn additional income after a reprimand. For Sassy: "With me or whatever, he'd pound the piss out of me but send me right back out." For Dee: "If he didn't think I made enough, he used to strip me down because he would think I was holding out on him." Wendy found herself in a toxic relationship with the man who housed her. She did not have intimate relations with him, but he dominated her, leading her to believe that she could not get along without him; when she refused to work, he hit her.

Lexus, Rianne, and Candy all reported that they had been beaten. Lexus recounted that once, when she was getting ready to leave, she was grabbed by the throat, dragged along the wall, and told in a menacing tone: "You are not leaving *this* family." This does not mean, however, that all workers were subjected to a manager's violence or passively submitted to his attempts at control. Reva and Chelsea, for example, were never beaten. Chelsea stated, "If someone told me you're not working, I'd say bye-bye. If he hit me, I'd hit him back." Coffee told us: "I usually take off and go to another small town or something like that and make my money … I would keep all the money, get my gram of weed, and he wouldn't know nothing about it."

Other acts of aggression were also reported. Rianne recounted angering her "man" when, after six sleepless nights, she fell into a deep sleep without having settled her account. She was brutally awoken when he started burning her with cigarettes. She then kicked him in the genitals and escaped. Rianne also emphasized that she generally defended herself against the exclusion that he employed by simulating indifference or by flirting with other people. Candy pretended that the blows did not hurt her and waited for an opportune moment to strike back. Reva admitted that she stole from her manager although she realized that this was very dangerous.

The Different Facets of Protection Offered by Street-Based Managers

In this section we look more specifically at the services offered by street-based managers to protect workers from physical assault, safeguard their physical and psychological health, and shield them from actions by law enforcement.

PROTECTION AGAINST CUSTOMERS' ASSAULTS

The managers told us that the measures they take include maintaining telephone contact with the worker before and after they rendezvous with clients, being visible on the street to encourage customers to behave properly, following the car that the worker has gotten into, waiting outside the room for the end of the rendezvous, and compiling a blacklist of bad customers. In the group interviews the workers confirmed that some of them coordinate with their manager to decrease their vulnerability to violence. Lily reported that she texts the destination and the time frame of her appointment and also uses the services of a contract third party: "I had this guy, and on X Street, there used to be a parking lot where we'd go to, but there would be a guy there who'd be protection, right? And he did give me a hard time. I had rolled down my window, and he did give me a hard time, and he had me like that. He smashed my head, and that guy was on him in two minutes."

Candy explained that the manager she works for keeps close track of her. To start with, he parks on the street in front of her, follows her movements, enters the hotel, and asks for the room number. Carissa reported that her partner forbids her from carrying a firearm for fear that the gun may be turned on her. He also refuses to work with her when she has been drinking because he feels that the work becomes too dangerous for her when she is impaired. Lexus reported that her manager protects her and taught her to defend herself against aggressive clients. She recounted the night a customer, a drug dealer and user, responded with violence when he discovered she was a trans woman. When he tried to stab her, her manager broke in through the door and hit the individual over the head with a chair. She then commented to Lexus that she could have done the same thing. From then on Lexus did not hesitate to fight back if she was assaulted. Chelsea noted that her manager-partner has a gun in the house, "just in case."

But not all managers offer such protection or the tools for workers to defend themselves; some simply wait for money and, as we saw in the previous section, can themselves be a source of violence. Wendy had such an experience: her first manager was a drug user who misrepresented himself as a dealer knowledgeable about sex work. He made himself visible on the street, but Wendy felt that this had the effect of repelling customers, who might have been scared of being robbed. Sometimes he hid in the bushes, and once, when Wendy did not return quickly enough from her rendezvous, he stood on the street corner – flashlight in hand – waiting. When she got out of the car, he pointed his flashlight towards it, leading the customer to believe it was a police officer and he would be arrested. Aside from monitoring her behaviour this individual took no other measures; he did not put customers on a blacklist and he did not react when Wendy reported wrongdoing. In Wendy's view: "He just wanted to have the money ... he didn't care about me." Other workers emphasized that with regard to safety, street-based work is teamwork; certainly the manager might be close by, but very often sex workers look out for each other. They write down a customer's licence plate number, keep track of where the car goes, and/or, at times, look into the customer's car and note his physical appearance. They might also warn a newcomer – this was Wendy's experience – that a customer presents risks and should be avoided: "This girl who's quite a bit bigger than both of us was like, 'What are you doing?' You know, like, 'I thought I told you to leave her alone,' and she actually confronted him. And I don't know why he was afraid of her. I know now that she's been on the streets quite a while, and I guess she had seniority. So he backed off." An experienced street-based worker also protected her one evening by confronting her manager, warning him he should leave Wendy alone if he did not want problems. In the end, sex workers helped Wendy escape his grasp; they were aided in part by the fact that, as he became increasingly dependent on drugs, he sent her to the street alone, affording her the opportunity to speak with women on the street and distance herself from him.

PROTECTION OF PHYSICAL AND PSYCHOLOGICAL WELL-BEING

In individual interviews with managers, some said that they purchase condoms for workers. When the interviewer mentioned this to the workers during the group interviews, the women's responses were both immediate and varied. Chelsea's, Rianne's, and Lexus's managers did nothing of the sort, whereas Lily was supplied with condoms and her doctor's appointments were booked. Candy reported that she was not only provided with condoms but also reminded to use them.

With regard to psychological well-being, the role of managers seems more limited. According to the workers interviewed, they were provided with drugs and money as needed, but were mainly reminded to bring back money. Rianne remarked that, after assisting/comforting her in a moment of distress, her manager told her that she was indebted to him and therefore required to bring in additional money. Lexus offered a different viewpoint: her manager taught her to assume control when negotiating services with her customers. With her encouragement she learned to refuse requests that made her uncomfortable and came to recognize that failure to do so is risky for her physical integrity, sexual health, and self-esteem.

PROTECTION AGAINST CRIMINAL INTERVENTION

In the individual interviews, the managers spoke of their concern that they would be denounced to the police by discontented sex workers. At the same time, they said that they do not physically abuse the workers. They also said that they are discreet so as not to draw attention and that they advise the workers to avoid very conspicuous clothing and to choose apparel appropriate for their place of work. Finally, they claimed that they protect the workers and themselves against police intervention by recording code names in their phones.

The workers, for their part, felt that managers are not at great risk of being arrested unless he or she lives in an area known for prostitution activity; there is a good deal of movement around their apartment; they talk too much; or are very violent towards a worker who would then have no choice but to turn to the authorities. For example, some workers, seeing that Wendy had been the victim of violence by her "pimp," reported the problem to the police. As a consequence, patrol officers began to ask her how she had received her injuries. As Wendy explained, "I was pretty bruised up and stuff a few times. Of course, the officers began to know me, and I had them pull up and say to me stuff like, 'Well, we know that he did this to you, and we heard,' you know, and I'd be like, 'Oh, where did you hear that?' And so he would name off a couple street girls, and – and, you know, rightfully, they're right." Wendy answered that a jealous girl had hit her but she was well aware that the officers had obtained the information from sex workers who wanted to protect her.

The workers also consider that the manager cannot truly protect them from the police when the latter set up sting operations and/or use entrapment. Nevertheless, he may quickly pay their bail. Candice, for example, reported that her third party had provided support and advice after her arrest and during the legal proceedings. Candy explained that her manager had taught her everything she needed to know to be safe: he told her about the police, about the street, where to go, and the places to avoid. And when he was arrested and charged, he made sure that someone would take care of her and that she would have a place to live.

Concluding Reflections

The focus-group interviews with street-based sex workers enabled us to paint a portrait of the manager's work that brings to light the difficulties associated with sex work in this sector and, especially, the variety of labour relations between managers and workers. In terms of both recruitment and the division of tasks and responsibilities, the options are quite diverse. Also revealed were various ways to divide income – linked more or less to the division of tasks – and the control exerted on a continuum from draconian to democratic. Finally, we examined the extent to which the street-based manager is able to protect the workers he or she manages.

We identified a certain number of factors that encourage female street-based sex workers to seek out or accept the protection of a manager. For those just starting out – who have little experience and are scared – the individual may offer some security against the unknown or against other, potentially hostile, sex workers. This was the case for Wendy, who, new to the world of street-based sex work, accepted for a period of time the protection of a drug user who encouraged her not to trust the other street-based workers. And yet, ultimately, these women were the ones who offered her support and in time enabled her to distance herself from this abusive relationship.

For those who choose to work on certain streets, a manager is, at times, the only social actor who has the authority to protect them against verbal abuse, physical assaults, and robbery. In these cases, he is an essential intermediary. In addition to protection, managers may offer other services. Depending on the workers' needs, he may supply beauty products or clothing for work, drugs, alcohol, and/or food. In this type of relationship, his or her responsibilities are diverse and the relationship clearly revolves around a business model in which each participates actively on a daily basis. Although the partnership is not egalitarian, it is not one in which the worker must silently accept a despotic abuser or violent reactions.

Finally, the manager may also be a spouse. In this case, each partner may have at heart the protection of the other and emotions colour the different aspects of the relationship. In Candy's case, this relationship made it possible to divide the heterosexual couple's tasks in a non-traditional way (the male spouse takes care of the children and she works out of the home) and at the same time redefine the traditional power relations between manager and street-based sex worker (she takes care of her own protection and worries that he will be arrested and charged with procuring).

In sum, our data shows that describing street-based managers solely according to notions of control and violence perpetrated on street-based sex workers obscures the complexity and types of relations that may develop between the two parties. In turn, this clarifies why many workers refuse to be defined and labelled as victims.

Notes

1 Gleeson (2004, 103) notes that "in different times and jurisdictions the *prostitute* has been targeted differently."
2 It should be noted that this research, based on a small sample of twenty-two individuals, suffers from a number of problems related to scientific validity. In fact, the category "procurer" does not refer to a homogeneous group but to a legal category comprised of persons who have been criminally charged. Furthermore, although Spidel et al. (2006) used a control group of prisoners not diagnosed as psychopaths, there was no control group of individuals who share the characteristics attributed to psychopaths but who have not necessarily broken, or been charged with breaking, the law.
3 Karandikar and Prospero, 2010; Miller, 1995; Norton-Hawk, 2004; Raphael and Powers, 2010; Raphael and Shapiro, 2004; Sanders, 2001; Silbert and Pines, 1981.
4 Dalla, 2002; Norton-Hawk, 2004; Raphael and Powers, 2010; Raphael and Shapiro, 2004; Sanders, 2001; Silbert and Pines, 1981.
5 See Introduction (this collection) for more information on the Management Project's research protocol.

4 The Business of Sex Businesses: Management in the Incall/Outcall Sector

CHRIS BRUCKERT AND TUULIA LAW

In this chapter we draw on interviews conducted with third parties and sex workers in the incall/outcall[1] sector as part of the Management Project to shed light on the business of sex businesses. Our focus is on the management of incall and outcall agencies, and the third parties who supervise, control, facilitate, and/or coordinate the labour process and/or practices of adult sex worker(s). Unlike contractor[2] and associate[3] relationships, where independent sex workers retain control over their labour process, in this arrangement the worker enters into an employee-like relationship with a third party who coordinates and facilitates the delivery of an erotic, sexual, or interpersonal service to clients. As the chapter will demonstrate, depending on the size of the agency management can be a collaborative effort by multiple third parties exercising various levels of oversight or specialization in regard to administering the business, or it can be the purview of one individual.

We start by considering the international literature on third parties in the incall and outcall sectors before examining the business of the Canadian commercial sex industry, attending to both organizational components (including marketing, branding, structure) and day-to-day operations (such as attracting and maintaining clients, ensuring quality service provision, training). We then move on to consider the reasons sex workers elect to work for a third party rather than set up their own business as independent entrepreneurs (or "independents"). In this section we see that while the third party–sex worker relationship is sometimes characterized by conflicting interests, third parties in the incall/outcall sector also provide a number of services some sex workers find useful. For example, they may facilitate access to customers, deal with clients, offer training and mentorship, take care of administration, organize transportation, screen clients, and provide security. As part of this discussion we examine the tensions between sex workers and third parties rooted in conflicting economic interests before concluding with a reflection on power and resistance in this sector of the sex industry. Throughout we will see that criminalization pushes third parties to implement policies and practices that operate against the interests of sex workers at the same time as it undermines sex workers' ability to lay claim to labour rights. Here, as elsewhere, our findings echo those of Solanna et al. (2015), who assert "criminalization creates situations that force managers to implement strategies that put sex workers at risk" (20; see also Benoit et al., 2014; Bowen, Bungay, and Zangger, 2015; Bruckert and Law, 2013; Gillies, 2013).

Managing Incall/Outcall Work: International Comparisons

We begin by supplementing the limited body of research on Canadian third parties in the indoor commercial sex industry (Benoit et al., 2014; Bowen, Bungay, and Zangger, 2015) with studies conducted with sex workers who work for or with these individuals (Gillies, 2013; van der Meulen, 2010; Currie and Gillies, 2006). We also position the conversation within the broader international scholarship on the roles of third parties in countries where sex work is regulated (see also Jeffrey, this collection). Juxtaposing the findings from our criminalized system against research on legalized regimes such as Germany (Kavemann and Rabe, 2007), Holland (Wagenaar et al., 2013), Switzerland (Büschi, 2010), and Nevada, USA (Brents and Hausbeck, 2005), as well as research coming out of New Zealand (Abel and Fitzgerald, 2010; Government of New Zealand, 2008; Mossman, 2010) – where sex work was decriminalized[4] in 2003 – helps tease out the impacts of criminalization. Quite simply, "even imperfect forms of regulation are better for the human rights of sex workers than the illegality that automatically comes with the prohibition of prostitution" (Wagenaar et al., 2013, 6).

So how do regulated regimes reduce violence and engender better physical and sexual health for sex workers? In these jurisdictions, unlike in Canada, sex workers and third parties can contact law enforcement without fear of legal repercussions; have safer-sex supplies openly available[5]; and employ visible security mechanisms, such as cameras and guards, to deter inappropriate client behaviour (Wagenaar et al., 2013; Abel and Fitzgerald, 2010; Mossman, 2010; Government of New Zealand, 2008; Brents and Hausbeck, 2005). Moreover, as Brents and Hausbeck (2005) note, security is a by-product of bringing the sex industry out of the shadows: "the real mechanisms for protection are working in a setting that allows constant public scrutiny of the behaviour of the customer before the actual paid party that makes client anonymity and easy exit difficult, and that provides a houseful of people just a flimsy door away from the prostitute-john interaction" (281). Not surprisingly, sex workers working in these more secure labour environments do not have to be perpetually vigilant, and therefore report less stress and anxiety at work (Brents and Hausbeck, 2005).

In legalized and decriminalized systems sex workers are also, in principle, less vulnerable to economic exploitation. For example, in New Zealand the *Prostitution Reform Act* of 2003 prohibits the use of security deposits and fines (Abel and Fitzgerald, 2010) and in Germany third parties are not allowed to negotiate financial transactions between sex workers and their clients (Kavemann and Rabe, 2007). That said, it would appear that as in any industry (e.g., restrictions on the taxi industry have historically reduced potential workplaces and diminished the ability of workers to negotiate) regulation can also create conditions that facilitate the exploitation of sex workers by third parties. In Nevada, for example, sex workers are required to work in managed settings for establishments that take a considerable portion of their earnings (Brents and Hausbeck, 2005) – an issue Leslie Jeffrey examines in detail in the concluding chapter of this collection, suggesting, "the end result can be the establishment of oligopolistic control over the industry which ... can act in many ways to limit and undermine sex workers' workplace rights" (125) and create a barrier to the establishment of small businesses, including those that are run by sex workers.

Moreover, the characterization of sex workers as contractors rather than employees (an issue we examine later in this chapter; see also Law, this collection) combined with bureaucratic indifference or a lack of official oversight, as we see in the Netherlands (Wagenaar et al., 2013), undermine sex workers' ability to assert their labour rights. Ultimately, regardless of regulatory regime, it would appear that in the sex industry, as in any other labour market sector, there are good and bad bosses (Büschi, 2010; Brents and Hausbeck, 2005). As this chapter will demonstrate, this is also the case in Canada.

Sample

The research protocol for the project was detailed in the Introduction. Here we present the characteristics of the subsample we draw on for this chapter. In total we interviewed 50 incall/outcall third parties, of whom 40 were women (including 2 women who were trans) and 10 were men. Of those 50 participants, 4 identified as Black, 2 as Asian, 39 as white, 4 as biracial, and one participant identified simply as "a woman of colour." Our sample varied widely in terms of age and experience; ages ranged from 24 to 62 years (with an average age of 38) and from 3 months to 20 years' experience working as third parties. Notably, only 7 had no experience as sex workers, and 17 had worked as a sex industry third party in more than one organization or capacity. Twenty-nine had also held managerial positions outside the sex industry, while only 2 participants had never worked in mainstream jobs. Although the level of education is not known for all the third parties we interviewed, 4 had graduate degrees, 11 had university degrees, 8 had college degrees, 11 had other post-secondary education, 4 had finished high school, and 5 had some high school education. This demographic profile challenges stereotypes of third parties as "shady characters" existing on the fringes of society, discussed in Chapter 2. While our focus in this chapter is on agencies (and hence the third parties who operate them), we also draw on the information provided by third parties who can be classified as associates or contractors (see Introduction) in the incall/outcall sector. These individuals are experts on the business of sex business by virtue of their third party work and, in many cases, their experience as sex workers.

These narratives are put in conversation with incall/outcall sex workers, who were interviewed in focus groups in Halifax (where 6 people participated), Toronto (11 participants in two focus groups), Ottawa (3), and Montreal (7). Of these 27 participants, all identified as women including 3 women who were trans. Three participants identified as Black, 3 as biracial, 2 as Indigenous, 16 as white, and 3 participants did not disclose their ethnicity. Focus-group participants' ages ranged from 21 to 57 years old, with 1 to 44 years experience in the sex industry. Notably, while participants had to select one focus group in which they could participate, many had laboured in various other sectors of the sex industry – 4 had worked on webcam, 8 had been erotic dancers, 6 had worked in the street-based sex industry, 1 had worked as an actress in pornography, and another had worked as an erotic phone-service attendant. In addition, a significant proportion (12) had been or were currently independent sex workers.

Sex Businesses: Commercial Enterprises
in the Shadow of Criminalization

Commercial sex businesses are exceedingly diverse. Not only do they range from small owner-operated establishments to large agencies with multi-tier management structures, but, as they endeavour to cater to an un/under-fulfilled demand or underserviced clientele, they vary widely in terms of the kinds of services offered (e.g., erotic massage, full service, "kink"); the location of the service encounter (e.g., brothel, hotel, dungeon, massage parlour); and brand or image. In the coming section we tease out the implications for sex workers when legal concerns – intersecting with market, personal, and economic considerations – play out in the shadow economy.

As in any commercial enterprise, third parties in the sex industry organize their business according to real or perceived markets as well as their interests, competencies, and motivation. That said, in a criminalized sector not only is market research not an option but legal considerations also condition the organization of the business. For example, some third parties keep their businesses small in order to avoid detection. As Adele (outcall agency owner, Montreal) told us, "I didn't want to have a lot of visibility and a lot of expansion. When you want to make more money, you risk not just losing your job, but you also risk being more visible, being spotted by the police."[6] In an effort to minimize the risk of criminalization many agency owners and managers also frame their enterprise in a manner that obscures the sexual nature of the services provided. Incall establishments are "massage parlours" and outcall agencies present the fiction that they are escort agencies organizing company only: "In the initial interview with the girl, when I would hire them, I wouldn't talk openly about sex ... We always had to run our business under the pretense of doing something else" (Joe, outcall agency owner, Toronto). How services are communicated can have a significant impact on the success of the business. Robin (sex worker, Toronto) compared two incall establishments employing different strategies in this regard: "The first place that advertised it as what it was, like, was pretty busy ... Lots of clients coming in all the time, and they knew ... what they were getting. And then the other place [that attempted to pass as an aromatherapy business] was really dead."

Even agencies that are open and forthright about the services they provide strive to advertise in such a manner as to avoid coming to the attention of law enforcement and/or producing evidence that could be used against them in court. Of course since December 2014 they would also be contravening *Criminal Code* section 286.4, which criminalizes advertising "an offer to provide sexual services for consideration." Many attempt to "stay under the radar" by being extremely vague in their advertisements; at the agency Trina (sex worker, Ottawa) worked at they were "very, very low-key, no pictures, very little information. So that was definitely a barrier because people would assume that we were a legitimate massage place, which was kind of frustrating and awkward." The common use of "code" to convey information discreetly can also result in miscommunication:

> You have to take "detours" in order to explain what the client can expect. So, there's the term *GFE*, "girlfriend experience," which, in the [industry] jargon, means particular services. So, the clients kind of know. But it also doesn't really mean anything [specific] – GFE isn't in the dictionary.[7] (Karolanne, outcall agency owner, Montreal)[8]

In any service business, it is not simply a question of *what* services are offered and the *context* in which the service encounter takes place but also to whom the service will be provided and by whom. Sex businesses adjust their branding according to the type of clients they wish to attract. For example, an "upscale" business will select a name and tag line that conveys exclusivity; use "classy" images and/or high-quality photographs; and position itself at the higher end of the market price range. By contrast, an agency like Lisa's (incall agency, Toronto), which strives to be "as accessible for someone who is working a $15-an-hour job as to someone who is working a $115-an-hour job," will cultivate a more "down to earth" image.

Bridget, a Jamaican-Canadian woman, illustrates how an agency's image and the clientele they want to attract conditions advertising but also affects hiring practices:

> I don't like young guys ... They have a sense of entitlement. A lot of times they're intoxicated, there's more than one, and they're egging each other on, so it's not really a great environment to be in. So I try to steer clear of the kids. I don't like to advertise in the younger sites. So I don't like to advertise young girls, like eighteen, nineteen, I don't like that demographic: a) I don't like that it attracts the younger guys, and b) I don't like the type of men that [are] attracted to young girls like that ... I like to stay in the twenty-two-and-older age bracket. I like affluent men; Caucasian, affluent men. I worked a lot in Ottawa, so we liked to target, like, MPs, government workers, things

like that. So we try to brand ourselves as elite, classy, so our girls would have names like Tiffany, Amber, Scarlet, just so we could attract those types of clients ... They tend to book for longer periods of time, they're safer, they have families, they have things to lose. They're not going to get us involved in any kind of bad situation. In terms of advertising ... if we had pictures in our advertisements, the girls were always in white garters or black stockings, and pearls. I'm really big on pearls in the ads.

Similarly, EJ, a Toronto-based massage parlour owner, is looking for workers who are attractive and "treat this job like they would treat any other job. So when you go in for an interview, you're dressed appropriately, you arrive on time or even a little bit early, that you ask questions." She also prefers workers who are in their late twenties or early thirties; she explains that the majority of her clients "want to be able to have a conversation with them. So if you really have no life experience under your belt, how can you really connect with a fifty-five-year-old man?" That said, in the sex industry maturity is relative: Joe (outcall agency owner, Toronto) would warn "older" women between the ages of thirty-five and forty-five that "in your age range, we're not that busy. We can maybe give you a call or two a week, but that's the maximum."

Moreover, while Bridget and EJ speak to a desire to hire "mature" sex workers with a middle-class presentation of self, Western standards of beauty favouring a white, slim, young, heteronormative appearance often condition hiring practices and, as we examine shortly, impose expenses on workers who must maintain a particular "look." As Miss W. (outcall agency manager, Montreal) explains, "We do have a lot [of clients] now who want models, like really model girls, very skinny. The clients seem to want skinnier and skinnier. We talk about it and we don't like it but what are we supposed to do?" Of course not all agencies limit themselves to this aesthetic; Zoe, herself a full-figured woman, has branded her business around (and therefore restricted her hiring according to) an altogether different look, hiring only "big beautiful women" or BBWs[9] – she even jokingly informed the interviewer that she was not voluptuous enough to work at her agency: "[a] pretty girl like you, you're too tiny."[10] However, for sex workers like Maxine (Ottawa) sizeism has economic consequences:

The parlour where I worked at didn't really cater to [a range of tastes]. They were more, like, into the stripper figure. So work was really hard to come by. I'd have weeks without work because the parlour didn't advertise my body type or whatever. They'd just be like, "Oh, yeah, and this is Maxine." You would get things like, "Well, she's a larger girl." Not, you know, "She's curvy."

In addition to sizeism and classism, racism also plays out in the clandestine space of the sex industry, particularly in the way the narrow framing of beauty intersects with perceptions of market demand (see also Bruckert and Parent, 2014; Bruckert and Law, 2013; Chapkis, 2000; Ross, 2009). While some agencies refuse to discriminate, a number of third parties spoke of having racial quotas. Moxie (sex worker, Halifax) had even encountered an agency owner who refused to hire any Black women at all, ostensibly because that was not what her clients wanted. Reflecting on her experience of racial bias, Toronto sex worker Lee recalls, "being told by agencies because I'm Black that I may not get calls, I'm not popular, I'm difficult to market. So my only way of combating that was to be available as much as I could." Sadly, that women who fall outside the narrow definition of (white) Western attractiveness – be they older, racialized, full-figured, or "alternative" – have fewer employment options is not unique to this labour sector. There is ample evidence of discriminatory hiring practices and "lookism" in the mainstream labour market (YWCA 2008). However, in the face of discriminatory employment practices, sex workers labouring in the shadow economy are denied access to even the limited recourse available to workers in the mainstream labour market.

Day-to-Day Business: Service Provision

As agency owners explained, running a small business – as in any sector of the labour market – is a lot of work. EJ, a massage parlour owner in Toronto, spoke of "getting in early, checking emails, putting ads up, doing the schedule, making sure that the place is clean, that we have supplies, planning events, parties, stuff like that." And Carole, another Toronto incall agency owner, noted "I start and finish the day with cleaning and laundry"; she is also "responsible for, like, everything in the house – for the cleaning, the shopping, the advertising, the photography, the editing of photos, the daily scheduling, and the liaising with clients." [11]

Evidently, as Carole alludes, a significant responsibility of third parties in the incall/outcall sector is booking clients, something that Miss W. (outcall agency owner, Montreal) explains can be "tough work ... I gotta make this fantasy come true or this nice experience for them ... It's not just me taking a call and sending a text, especially if there's a lot of email back and forth between the client and me." As service-provision businesses, agencies must not only promote their business to attract customers but also build and maintain their clientele. To this end they must strive to "match" clients to the appropriate service provider, "getting someone who actually works for [the client] ... Really listening to what the guys were wanting" so that "the clients are happy, the girls are happy, and the owner is happy" (Jackie, receptionist, Toronto). Beatrice, the owner of a large escort agency in Hamilton, explains the hidden work that ensures the seamless delivery of services:

> I have got three core people that work under me ... Their responsibilities are answering the telephones, coordinating appointments, making sure that the girls have signed on, that the girls have signed off, that the drivers have had all of the proper information dispatched over to them, etcetera, etcetera. We use software to be able to make sure we've got everything timing-wise, because in a given day we've got so many appointments that it does get very, very confusing. Well when you've got about fifty appointments happening it tends to be in usually about a six-hour time span, usually between about 6 pm to 12 am ... I'd say that it's probably as close to air-traffic control as it can possibly get.

In any service-market businesses (including the sex industry) there is no tangible product and instead "services disappear at the point of consumption and they cannot be processed ... [moreover] production and consumption of a service are usually simultaneous and inseparable" (Doyle, 2011, 244). Confronted with the intangibility and inseparability of production and consumption, incall or outcall agencies must not only promote and attract clients but also endeavour to ensure that their customers receive "good service."[12] Since third parties are not present during service delivery they endeavour to ensure quality service provision at a distance by imposing expectations on workers according to the image, branding, services, and organizational structure of the agency. Commonly, this includes: being punctual and professional (e.g., no "attitude"); being a conscientious service provider (e.g., spending the agreed-upon period of time with the client); and respecting other "house rules," including workplace etiquette (e.g., no smoking, no consuming alcohol or drugs, maintaining standards of cleanliness). Christina (sex worker, Toronto) "got emailed a list of about, you know, four pages of procedures and what's expected of you ... How you were expected to dress, you know, whether or not you should work when you're on your period – the answer was 'no.' " Many agencies require workers to adopt a presentation of self in keeping with the agency image (e.g., clothing, make up, cleanliness). For example Alex, who worked for an upscale escort agency in Toronto, was to look "professional ... like a sexy businesswoman. But not too sexy."

Many businesses instruct the people they hire to ensure they represent the business in the "right" way. Here again we see how this quite conventional expectation takes on distinct characteristics in the sex industry. Mielle, an outcall agency owner in Ottawa, informed sex workers about the procedures and precautions they should follow in relation to the criminalized context: "I explain the breakdown of the law to them. I explain what they're going to be doing. I explain to them the procedure for collecting money." Sophie (incall/outcall agency owner, Ottawa) employed a more "hands-on" approach, bringing new hires with her on calls to train for two weeks. Training becomes particularly important if the services offered are more specialized; for example, at the dungeon where Kitty (sex worker) worked in Toronto, "usually everybody started out submissive ... And then if you were going to be using implements, then somebody would have to show you how to use a flogger or a cane and where to hit ... You don't hit where the kidneys are." However, as we will see throughout this chapter, sometimes what third parties perceive to be worthwhile is perhaps less effective than they imagine. Alana (sex worker, Ottawa) describes her "training" as being "thrown into a training session with someone else who really wouldn't show you what you were supposed to be doing." Of course the laws provide a powerful disincentive for managers to provide important training for fear "of being mistaken for procuring" (Pierrette, sex worker and personal assistant, Ottawa).

While agencies are, at least in our research, respectful of sex workers' boundaries regarding the specific sexual services they will (and will not) provide, they may insist on safety protocols and mandatory condom use, as Joe (outcall agency owner, Toronto) explains:

> If I found that a girl was not using condoms, I would just say to her that, "I understand you're not," and warn her that she should. And, if I continuously found that she wasn't, then, I'd have to let go of her. Because then the other girls on staff would be pressured into not using condoms, from customers.

Though such regulations can be frustrating, they can also be useful. For example, a strict "no barebacking" (sex without a condom) policy is a resource sex workers told us they evoke to insist clients respect their safer-sex boundaries. Similarly "being at the agency where you have to call in and confirm that the money was there made it a lot easier to collect and to talk about money" (Eva, sex worker, Toronto).

What happens when workers fail to meet the expectations of the agency or respect the codes of conduct in the incall/outcall sector? While some third parties impose fines – a practice that would not be tolerated in mainstream labour sectors – most use very conventional strategies, including verbal reprimands, warnings, temporary suspensions, and in the case of Carole, an incall agency owner in Toronto, "a furrowed brow." Sex workers who are repeatedly unavailable when called (after having accepted a shift) or late may be allocated less work:

> How much work you got that evening was determined by how flipping on time you were for the calls and how quickly you responded to them. If you showed me in two different calls that you were going to be late and I had to deal with customers saying, "Where is she? Where is she?" you absolutely would get dropped to the bottom ... You're just, like, slowing shit down and also bringing a bad name – rap – to the organization, the agency. (Kaya, receptionist, Toronto)

Rules governing things like punctuality also work in the interests of sex workers, whose income may also suffer if the agency earns a reputation for not respecting customers' time and expectations. Sandra (sex worker, Toronto) explained why she supported not only the rule but the sanctioning of her colleagues who failed to comply:

> If you don't come out of the calls in an hour, or at the end of it, if it's two hours or whatever. If you do have a driver on multiple calls it can screw everything up because they have to go pick someone else up at the end of her hour. So I actually found when they implemented the fines – and it's a minor, minor fine – but it made a huge difference because it made it more efficient for the rest of us. So that we weren't stranded because a driver had to wait fifteen minutes extra for her, and then you're waiting fifteen minutes extra at your call.

As Sandra's comments show us, in addition to efficiency and the agency's reputation, good time management impacts sex workers' safety (they do not have to wait in an unfamiliar neighbourhood). Unlike the practices we saw in Chapter 3, incall and outcall sex workers who consistently fail to meet the expectations of agencies are fired: "I'd talk to them a few times, and if they wouldn't listen, they'd have to be let go" (Ava, incall agency owner, Toronto). Importantly, in a criminalized context sex workers are denied redress through labour laws, an issue we will return to shortly.

Why Work for an Agency?

The challenges and expectations detailed above beg the question: *Why would someone work for a third party?* This is particularly salient in the current context: technological innovations – most notably the Internet and cellular phones – have not only transformed sex industry practices but have also enabled sex workers to work as "independents" by advertising online and going about their daily tasks while maintaining contact via cell phones and email (Bernstein, 2007b).

Sex workers told us that being an "independent" entails running a business, which necessitates skills (e.g., business, organization, public relations), assets (e.g., cell phone, a steady Internet connection, an appropriate location or at least a credit card to book hotel rooms for incall work), knowledge (e.g., security strategies, how to organize photo shoots), as well as time and labour (e.g., to place ads, answer emails). Some sex workers do not have the money to start and maintain their own business; others lack the time, interest, or competence to assume responsibility for wide-ranging administrative tasks. Trina, an Ottawa-area sex worker explains that third parties "were in charge of paying the bills, cleaning – like, all of the day-to-day operations that I may not want to deal with." She goes on: "I found working for a third party was so much more simple. You came in, you left, and you brought your money with you. But being independent, you're working all of the time, you're constantly answering emails, cleaning your location, shopping for new things."

Trina alerts us that having someone undertake tasks perceived to be distasteful contributes to the maintenance of a healthy work-life balance; additionally, some sex workers felt it was – somewhat surprisingly, given that agencies take between 30 and 50 per cent of the service fees – in their financial interests as well (see also

Gillies, 2013). Agencies obtain clients: "Ultimately, their job is to get you business, and by getting you business, they get business" (Christina, sex worker, Toronto). This allows the worker to "actually make money rather than going out and having to put yourself out there and do the marketing and do everything you need to do to make the money. You can say, 'Okay, you know what – you've done this for me. Now I can just do my job' " (Rose, sex worker, Toronto). Rebecca (Montreal) explained: "The agency I'm working for at the moment, it's 50 per cent [cut] with the driver fees [included]. And, at first, I thought, 'Is this really fair? Is this really what I want?' But this agency, they negotiate higher prices,[13] so I have more money in my pocket anyway. So, I am happy with that."[14]

In short, third parties offer concrete benefits. This is in contrast to the state's supposition that such arrangements are "so inherently damaging and exploitative as to require blanket prohibition" (Gillies, 2013, 271). It would appear that sex workers make the same sort of decisions as workers in mainstream labour sectors. The analogy here is simple – some plumbers start their own small businesses, others prefer not to invest the capital, time, and energy into branding, advertising, purchasing tools and a work vehicle, bidding on jobs, and billing clients; others simply lack the skills or motivation or interest to manage their own business. In any case, these tradespeople elect to work for someone else. There is, however, a significant difference, one that would not factor in the cost-benefit analysis of a plumber – criminalization. In a criminalized and stigmatized industry, sex workers are hesitant to contact the police (Krüsi et al., 2014; Bruckert and Chabot, 2010; Jeffrey and MacDonald, 2006; Lewis and Shaver, 2006) – in this context the security third parties offer takes on particular significance.

Safety, Security, and Managing Workplace Risks

The sex workers we spoke with appreciated the security that working for a third party afforded them: according to Sandra (sex worker, Toronto), "it's absolutely safer, I think, when you're working in a network of people" (see also Bowen, Bungay, and Zangger, 2015; Solanna et al., 2015, Benoit et al., 2014, Krüsi et al., 2012). In fact, while not compelled by occupational health and safety regulations (from which the sex industry is de facto excluded), safeguarding the well-being of sex workers is, as Halifax brothel operator Horeta explains, both a professional obligation and in the self-interest of third parties: "I was very particular about making sure that the girls were safe for two reasons – one, because of the girl and because I had been in her position [as a sex worker]; two, because that kind of shit brings heat on your business." The potential business costs of failing to create a safe working space, highlighted by Brents and Hausbeck (2005) in their study of legalized brothels in Nevada, are applicable to criminalized spaces as well:

> It is never in the business interests of brothel owners to have an environ-ment of fear or danger permeating the exchanges in their bordellos. Such a climate works against the ability to hire motivated and hard-working prostitutes, generates concern among local officials and regulatory bodies, which therefore could threaten licensing, and poisons relations with cus-tomers looking for a good time, not a dangerous liaison. (277)

In an effort to reduce the likelihood that a sex worker will confront an unsafe situation, agencies may implement zero-tolerance policies and/or maintain "bad client" lists; many rely heavily on the collection of personal information to deter clients from acting inappropriately:

> That's always something that people come to me at first and they're like, "What happens if the guy hurts me?" It's like, well, this is an outcall situa-tion so we know where the person lives, and even if they rent a hotel, even if they book with a false name, there's a credit card and driver's licence that's on file ... With an agency there are so many people that know exactly where that girl is at any given time. (Beatrice, outcall agency owner, Hamilton)

In addition to the mode of deterrence that Beatrice describes above, agencies also use this information to screen out potentially problematic clients based on experience, perception, prejudice, or intuition. The lat-ter, which as Rhonda (workplace provider, Toronto) pointed out "doesn't just come out of nowhere, even though sometimes it feels like it does," speaks to the sex work experience many agency owners and manag-ers bring to their third party work. For example, outcall agencies may consider specific spaces (e.g., basements) and/or geographic locations (e.g., particular neighbourhoods) to be "risky." Given the preoccupation with potential criminal charges, screening is not only about eliminating potentially aggressive clients, but also about avoiding being criminally charged. In this context there is always the possibility that, preoccupied with ensuring the prospective client is not a police officer (e.g., Are they asking too many questions? Are they being too explicit on the phone?), the third party will "miss" other significant indicators of risk.

The sex workers we spoke with felt that the collection of information and screening of potential clients were decidedly useful services. That said, it is important to recognize that while some agencies rigorously implement security protocols, sex workers were dubious that all agencies were consistently conscientious. Trina (Ottawa) was "sent on calls where the client was incredibly, like, stoned, or he was, you know, not making sense. And I mean the owner had taken the phone call for the call and should have been able to verify that. And this is someone who says that they screen their clients extensively."

Security may entail hiring other third parties such as, in the case of outcall agencies, drivers. Sylvia (outcall agency owner, Hamilton) explains that she had "a driver that I worked with. He was really good. He was really reliable. He'd drive them to their calls. He'd phone. He'd make sure that everything was cool, you know what I mean. If there was any problems, he would come to the door." The effectiveness of this strategy pivots on the driver's diligence and the agency's policies: "I mean in theory, I have a driver, but he doesn't actually wait around. He just goes off to drive someone else or drop someone else off and then just comes back at the end of the call. So if I text or whatever and everything's okay and suddenly, things go wrong, he's not actually there" (Alana, sex worker, Ottawa).

Many outcall agencies also require workers to call the agency when they arrive at the appointment. According to Christina (sex worker, Toronto) the procedure "did make me feel safe ... It was nice to know that there was somebody there waiting for me at the end of the call" – although she noted that remembering to phone could be "a small inconvenience. You get up to the client's house or hotel and sometimes you can get carried away, and you forget to call. And they start calling you like crazy. And sometimes, I already put my phone on vibrate, so that can be an issue."

Incall agencies employ different security protocols, oriented towards minimizing the likelihood of an aggressor entering the establishment. Lisa (incall agency owner, Toronto) had a particularly elaborate procedure:

> They would book a call and then have to confirm half an hour before coming over. And then I would direct them to where they could park in that vicinity, in that area, and direct them to a payphone that they would have to call me from down the street. I had all the payphone numbers memorized so I was able to know they were actually there. And then at that point I would give them the building address and the buzz code, and I

could monitor them through the TV down in the lobby. It wasn't until they actually rang up that they got the number itself. So I felt that any predator type of person wouldn't go through all those stops, all those hurdles, all those hoops, in order to get to myself or one of the other women, right. They tend to prey on the weak or the more vulnerable.

Incall agencies may also employ deterrence tactics, including on-call or on-site security staff or the creation of a "virtual" bouncer to produce the illusion of security personnel. For example, Zoe, who runs a midsized brothel in Québec City, keeps a pair of men's shoes visible at the entrance. More frequently, incall agencies rely on the same strategy as retail establishments when they schedule additional staff on night shifts – the presence of others to deter clients from acting inappropriately or aggressively. At small incall agencies this may be the owner-operator, other sex workers, or the receptionist. This also ensures that, should aggressors not be deterred, intervention can be swift. Horeta, a brothel manager in Halifax, reminisced about her time as a sex worker:

> I remember one day at the Cat's Meow we heard this slap, and this is in-service, so you very seldom ran into violence. But I heard this slap, so of course, every woman in the place has got one shoe off, and we're at the door. Ready to punch his ... we all wore steel-shank stilettos, you know, the weapon you can carry and no one can charge you with.

Although in this criminalized industry third parties and sex workers are anxious about law enforcement, it is important to note that some third parties will nonetheless call the police if a sex worker is in a dire situation. Andrew (outcall agency owner, Montreal) telephoned law enforcement when a client was being violent towards an escort, and indeed the police responded swiftly after he reminded them that it would be much messier if he called upon his own security to deal with it. Similarly, according to Joe (outcall agency owner, Toronto), "they [the police] really don't care much as long as you don't start solving the problems yourself." Carole, a Toronto incall agency owner, was also "not afraid to call the cops if we need to ... The protection of the individuals here is the number one goal."

Tensions and Conflicting Interests

To this point we have seen that agencies are direct-service businesses that operate on the same principles as other commercial enterprises – they brand themselves and endeavour to attract and maintain a regular clientele. To this end they advertise, hire service providers that reflect their image, and impose codes of conduct on workers. We have also seen that commercial sex agencies provide important business and security services that sex workers appreciate. This is not to say that all third parties are ethical business people who operate in the interests of the sex workers they hire.[15] Indeed, while the relationship can be mutually beneficial, it is perhaps not surprising that the agency's goal of generating a profit while avoiding criminal sanction are, at times, in conflict with sex workers' desire to do the same. As Benoit et al. (2014) remind us, "tensions involving sellers, buyers and managers occur in the sex industry, but they are not endemic" (iv).

As we have already noted, the issue of safety and security is sometimes contentious. In an effort to maximize income some third parties may "cut corners" and be less than diligent in regard to screening. Notably, in spite of third party shortcomings sex workers' security may nonetheless be enhanced in a collective environment: "Working in massage places, we did do a buddy system … We just did it as sisters working together. It had nothing to do with management" (Moxie, sex worker, Halifax). Rather obviously, the mere presence of others deters wrongdoing and increases workers' feeling of security.

There is also the issue of uncompensated labour. Agencies, in an effort to minimize costs, may expect workers to take on work-related tasks in the form of cleaning, laundry, and receptionist duties. Since workers are not paid by the hour, this amounts to agencies demanding "free" labour. Alana (sex worker, Ottawa) found herself paying a cleaning fee for a task she herself was doing. Trina, also from Ottawa, did more wide-ranging (uncompensated) tasks that put her at risk of being charged under the procuring provisions (formerly s. 212(1), now s. 286.3) of the *Criminal Code*: "Some of the girls would answer the phone. At some point, I would be managing the place out of default because I was the most senior girl there. So I would be answering the phones and doing the bookings, but I wasn't getting paid for it."

Sex workers also told us that expectations regarding self-presentation and maintenance sometimes pose a financial hardship. Lee (sex worker, Toronto) recounted:

> I met with an agency owner, and I didn't have the professional image that she wanted. I had to cash out my RRSP to make that image … They're telling me to look a certain way; they're not understanding that if they want my hair to look all that silky and smooth, it's $300, when some days, I'd barely make $80 if I'm lucky, if it's a half-hour call. So it just became a big, huge struggle of maintaining their image.

Lee's narrative also speaks to the additional expense, time, and effort – spending hundreds of dollars for "silky and smooth" hair – that Black women have to put into meeting the (white) Western aesthetic that a number of agencies in our research favour.

Industry practices around communication with clients are additional sources of potential conflict. Agencies make their money on the number of service encounters. In their desire to secure a booking some agencies are less than truthful, leaving the sex worker to deal with disappointed clients. Kayla (sex worker, Halifax) speaks of her experience:

> A guy will call, and you know, "What type of girls do you have?" and they basically give a description of every girl that's working. However, the descriptions are never the truth … I was, like, probably about 145, and you see my hair's far from blonde, but they're advertising me as a blonde, 125 pounds, busty. So then, of course, they pick me. And then I get to the room, and the gentleman's like, "Well, you're not blonde," and I'm like, "No, by no means." And he's, you know, "You're not 125 pounds." "No, by no means."

Other sex workers described a distribution of clients that failed to take into account the needs of individual sex workers because "they're going to get their money anyway, whether it's five clients for one girl, one for another, they're still getting six clients' money. So they don't care" (Moxie, sex worker, Halifax). As Moxie goes on to explain, the issue of charging for "extras" (additional services) or accepting tips can be another source of disagreement: "They didn't want you asking for tips because they wanted the volume of clients. They didn't care how much money you made because if it was a tip, they get the same amount of money anyway."

Finally, some sex workers expressed concerns that while agency owners like Carole (Toronto) are committed to "protect[ing] myself and my staff" from criminal charges, other third parties endeavour to shield themselves by off-loading legal liability onto those who work for them. Horeta (outcall agency owner, Halifax) explains that in her agency sex workers "had to sign a contract at the time saying that they were not hired for sex. That way, if a young lady did happen to get arrested, only she would get arrested." At agencies where third parties are attempting to protect themselves from legal consequences through wilful blindness (to the provision of sexual services), safer-sex supplies are not provided and workers are required to be extremely discreet about storage and disposal of these provisions (see also Bowen, Bungay, and Zangger, 2015). This also means that sex workers cannot talk to other workers, or third parties, about the challenges they confront in their work, including inappropriate behaviour by customers. In wilfully blind agencies[16] workers must also negotiate services and compensation with clients, some of whom may sincerely believe the door fees are inclusive of sexual services. Trina, who worked for one such massage parlour in Ottawa, explained that:

> The client would pay a door fee upon arriving, so the owner was guaranteed their money, but then you would have to negotiate in-room as to what you would offer and what the payment would be ... You would agree to a price, do the session – at the very end, "Oh, well, I only have this much money on me," or "Oh, I thought the price you quoted me included the door fee, which I've already paid." So if I told them $100, they assume that they were only paying $50. And so I would often go through sessions and receive less money than what I had agreed to.

This reminds us that while tensions between sex workers and agencies are based on competing financial interests (and of course sometimes a decided lack of professionalism), operating in the shadow of criminalization impacts not only advertising and forthright engagement with clients, but may also increase sex workers' vulnerability to violence and workplace exploitation. It also inhibits security protocols, as Miss W. (Montreal, outcall agency manager) explains: "I would love to offer way more. I would love to have a driver. And security, like, have someone downstairs at all times for the appointment. I would love to keep really great client records and not worry about them getting stolen or used against me."[17] In addition, criminalization conditions power relations between third parties and sex workers, an issue to which we now turn.

Power, Resistance, and the "Employment" Relationship

Third parties' authority over sex workers is conditioned by their employment relationship. Although Lewis et al. (2003) distinguish between employees, who have a contract *of* employment/service, and those contracted *for* services, who are normally thought of as self-employed, they argue that this distinction is becoming nebulous, especially with the growth of non-standard and precarious labour.

Self-employment can be further divided between independent contractors, who own their own means of production, and dependent contractors, who rely on employers and are subject to their control but with little recourse (as compared to employees) against unfair labour conditions (Fudge et al., 2003; see also Vosko, MacDonald, and Campbell, 2009; Vosko, Zukewich, and Cranford, 2003). In mainstream labour sectors a person who has a home day care would constitute the former, while a taxi driver who rents his or her licence from the taxi company would be classified as the latter (Fudge et al., 2003).

While according to these definitions sex workers are certainly self-employed, it becomes difficult to discern whether they are independent or dependent contractors; they, of course, have sovereignty over their own bodies, which are the means of production in service provision, but at the same time they rely on the third parties with whom they work to provide clients, advertising, security, and a location. This distinction remains elusive for workers across the labour force (Fudge and Vosko, 2001) – so much so that one proposed solution has been to abandon this distinction altogether in favour of the more general term "worker," which would extend protection by "cover[ing] every work relationship that is characterised by dependency on the putative employer" (Davidov, 2005, 57).

How did our participants make sense of this relationship? Although some sex workers resist the framing of agencies as employers by insisting that agency owners "work for us, not the other way around" (Alana, sex worker, Ottawa), owners and managers treat sex workers as if they are employees who can be hired and fired (or, if found not to have the "right" look, or deemed unable to handle the job, not hired at all). In effect, then, the incall/outcall sex workers with whom we spoke are dependent contractors insofar as they usually work exclusively for one establishment;[18] they are not paid a wage/salary but relinquish a portion of their fees (between 30 and 50 per cent in our research) to the agency upon which they rely for the location, equipment, and clients.[19] As such, these sex workers occupy the same contradictory labour location as many ostensibly self-employed workers in the mainstream economy – including, for example, hair stylists, who can choose between relinquishing a portion of their earnings to the salon management who takes care of booking appointments and advertising, or renting a space in a salon and taking care of these tasks themselves (see Gonzales, 2010). Indeed while the former resembles an agency relationship, we also found arrangements comparable to the latter in the sex industry:

third parties who rent space in an incall location to "independent" sex workers (Bruckert and Law, 2013).

In the sex industry the situation is further complicated in a criminalized context where there can be no industry standards (see Jeffrey, this collection), so that new workers "don't even know what to expect" (Christina, sex worker, Toronto). On the one hand managers are unable to establish clear workplace rules: "It's just this trust that we have to have between each other, this mutual trust that they're going to do what they're supposed to do. We can't have a contract, so there's no laws, we can't sign a workers' agreement" (Miss W., outcall manager, Montreal). As we will soon see, this can result in workers resisting and behaving in ways that would not be acceptable in labour sectors where workers can be held to explicitly articulated occupational roles and expectations (see also Law, this collection). In short, criminalization inhibits the development of industry standards – something that would be in the interests of managers, clients, and workers. It also excludes sex workers from legal protection and safeguards, as Gillies (2013) persuasively argues:

> Unlike other workers ... sex workers are unable to reduce exploitation or seek redress through labour or employment laws. This is due to the doctrine of paramountcy, which gives federal laws, including the criminal sanctions against procuring, precedence over provincial laws such as labour, employment, and human rights legislation. (274)

As such, sex workers have no legal recourse against wrongful dismissal, arbitrary and undeserved disciplinary or labour practices (e.g., unfavourable scheduling for people the owner does not like), or sexual harassment from third parties. Moreover, sex workers are denied the protection afforded by provincial occupational health and safety legislation or federal statues like the *Human Rights Act*. They are also unable to organize into labour associations to protect their interests, as Leda (sex worker, Toronto) makes clear: "Unfortunately, with this kind of workplace situation, there is no union or, you know, guidelines that they have to follow, right, so it's really hard because sometimes, you get the short end of the stick."

Deprived of the ability to organize and/or turn to labour and human rights law when they face unfair labour practices sex workers in the incall/outcall sector nonetheless exert agency. Sometimes sex workers like Lee "protest with their feet" and simply remove their labour power: "I eventually quit and went to the competitive agency." This can be an effective strategy – after all, a service-provision agency is dependent on having service providers! Of course resigning is not necessarily desirable or financially viable for all sex workers, especially those whose employment options are limited by an appearance that does not meet (white) Western beauty ideals; these workers use the tools at hand to resist and subvert unfair labour policies.

At times resistance means creatively circumventing the rules. For example, when Moxie (sex worker, Halifax) was told she could not ask for tips she "would say [to clients], 'The nicer you are to me, the nicer I can be to you.' " She also colluded with regular clients, explaining that: "After a while, the clients got to know, well, that if you're only here for a short bit, pay for the half hour, tip me, and you get the hour service." Another covert resistance tactic facilitated safer sex practices. For example, because her workplace did not allow the conspicuous use of condoms, Diana (sex worker, Montreal) "used a box of Kleenex that … wasn't Kleenex. We put it all in there."[20] Faced with an inappropriate demand during an interview from an agency owner who "hinted that he would have liked a free service. And I know – I have personally met – the girls working for the agency who did do service for free," Christina (sex worker, Toronto) "pretended I didn't know what he was talking about."

Sex workers also build alliances in order to undermine managerial authority. Some, like Kayla (Halifax), foster relationships with support staff in order to thwart the prohibition against asking for tips: she would purposely "get in pretty good with the receptionist … That way, she would always have my back." Other times these alliances are with co-workers. Indeed, in the absence of the ability to formally organize into labour associations, worker solidarity emerges as an important precondition to collective action:

> Sometimes, it's just talking with some of the other workers and building solidarity, like, "Did this happen to you?" Like just sort of checking in, like, "This isn't targeted towards me specifically; is this towards everybody?" And maybe, you know, we would talk about ways, like, "Should we talk to this person? Maybe let's talk to the drivers. Let's see what we can do." (Alex, sex worker, Toronto)

Alex went on to describe a successful collective intervention: "In the incall, basically, we decided that we were charging too much. So we just talked amongst ourselves – the workers – and we said, 'We're going to work for this, so advertise this,' and she's like, 'Okay, well, you know, I'll listen to you guys because you're the ones who are doing the work.' " Moxie (sex worker, Halifax) noted that sometimes sex workers would subvert managerial authority by working together to ensure a more equitable distribution of income: "The girls will say, 'Well, you know what? Like, I already had four clients, man – you ain't got one.' So if we get to answer the phones, we would push the girl who didn't get a client, you know? We would do that."

Awareness that they are valuable workers emboldens some sex workers to forthrightly contest workplace expectations. For Alana (Ottawa) this meant telling her boss that it was her "choice to decide what I charge extra for"; Christina (Toronto), having unsuccessfully challenged the "not charging for extras" policy, took a less forthright approach and "just decline[ed] outright the extra service to clients." Other sex workers draw on their social capital to exert their rights. For Trina (Ottawa), this meant casually telling her boss that she was a member of the Ottawa-area sex worker rights group POWER, and asking "innocent questions when I started at first, like 'How would it work if we were paid per hour?' or 'What is it like for benefits? Do we have options for benefits?' " She explained, "the fact that I knew my rights, more or less, she knew that she couldn't take more advantage of me than she already was. She knew that I wouldn't do laundry if I didn't have a client. So she knew that if I had these boundaries and I stuck to them, that she couldn't do anything about it." Her knowledge and confidence also positioned Trina to mobilize her co-workers and effectively fight the owner's plan to "start holding onto the money and pay us out at the end of the week" – an action that highlights the importance of worker solidarity and collective action.

These acts of resistance not only illuminate sex workers' agency, they also draw attention to the complexity of power relations in this stigmatized and criminalized sector. Worker resistance occurs in a particular context, one in which managers endeavour to implement rules in the (sometimes conflicting) interests of their business and the health and safety of the sex workers they employ – all while avoiding criminal sanction. They are also motivated to retain staff, not only in the interests of providing a consistent service to customers but also to avoid hiring (a process that can result in procuring charges). They are also mindful that workers may switch agencies or work as "independents." Accordingly, there is a certain tolerance of work practices that would be unacceptable in mainstream labour sectors and an open acknowledgement that sometimes the work feels "like herding cats" (Beatrice, outcall agency owner, Hamilton). Nor will criminal behaviour be pursued, as Joe matter-of-factly explained: "If the girls steal money from you, let them take it. Don't go after them … It's not worth the trouble." Here we see that the criminal law (in particular CC s. 286.2 and 286.3) affords disgruntled former employees a powerful retaliatory weapon – albeit one that current employees are, for obvious reasons, unlikely to use. Brenda, the manager of a collective agency in Toronto, expressed the following concerns:

> One girl in the past who, I just couldn't believe her behaviour and I didn't even know how to deal with it … I was actually afraid of her to a point … if I tell her to leave, I don't know what she's going to do. I figured there'd be a chance that she would call the police on me. My biggest fear was the fact that, because of the laws, she could have ratted me out and then I would be screwed. And all the girls who are working with me would be screwed.

In this context forthright engagement is risky: "If someone fucks up – this is the way that I deal with conflict in the sex industry. And I kind of hate it but it's the safest. I don't openly invite conflict. And if somebody pisses me off, or I don't trust them anymore, I phase them out. I don't tell them openly, 'This is the issue' " (Rhonda, workplace provider, Toronto).

Criminalization also undermines open communication and solidarity among third parties. Here we see parallels between agency third parties and associates who provide incall locations. Lilith (Ottawa), who rents out her incall space and mentors another sex worker, explained that "it can create a really catty atmosphere that's really unfortunate … Someone who knows that I do massage and knows my address has a lot of power over me to really fuck over my life, whereas if I worked any other job, people wouldn't have that power over me. So the fact that we have so much power over each other … can create negative relationships." In other words, a dearth of industry standards means that competition between businesses is not only unregulated but can also result in criminal (or municipal) sanction, in turn impacting both third parties and sex workers (who would lose their workplace/space).

Concluding Reflections

Throughout this chapter we have seen that the organization of incall/outcall businesses, and the roles of third parties, resemble mainstream sectors of the labour market. We have seen that, shorn of moral outrage and absent salacious framing, management in the sex industry, like management in other sectors, is rather banal. Like mainstream business operators, third parties in the incall/outcall sector face challenges inherent to running a business: they juggle multiple tasks and responsibilities, from cleaning to organizing appointments to providing security measures. At the same time, however, their work is impacted by criminalization. Third parties cannot advertise or expand their businesses like enterprising operators do in other sectors, nor can they communicate openly with clients about services; in turn this lack of forthright engagement with clients, as well as wilful blindness, poses financial and security risks to sex workers. That said, third parties do provide security measures within these constraints; these strategies include screening clients (which is sometimes derailed by a concern about whether or not these individuals are police officers), noting clients' personal information, only releasing details about the service location when clients are nearby, and through actual and virtual security personnel. We have also seen that they draw on strategies used in mainstream businesses: these include having a number of workers on site to deter (or react to) customer misbehaviour, and in some instances, calling the police.

Third parties' relationship to sex workers is also impacted by criminalization. As de facto employers they want reliable workers but without written contracts or (in many cases) training, but have to accept the level of reliability that workers are willing to accede. Faced with unreliable workers, agency third parties must balance the legal risks posed by hiring (which can be construed as procuring) and firing (which opens up the possibility that workers will use the laws for retaliation) with the financial interests and reputation of the agency. At the same time, because criminalization excludes sex workers from provincial occupational health and safety laws, as well as federal labour and human rights provisions, it also limits the resistance strategies sex workers can draw upon.

Some of the conflict between third parties and sex workers that we have seen in this chapter emanates from their "employment" relationship. Absent from the service interaction, third parties cannot guarantee that workers will comply with rules and expectations in their behaviour towards clients, and, as we have seen, workers may take advantage of third parties' absence by disregarding policies governing the acceptance of tips and the provision of "extras." Such challenges posed by the direct and unsupervised interaction between customers and workers are not unique to the sex industry: they are in fact inherent to management in the service sector writ large (see Bolton and Houlihan, 2010). That said, sometimes it appears that third parties make use of their absence in the service interaction to misrepresent the sex worker to the client, leaving the sex worker to manage the client's surprise or disappointment. It is here that we see that industry standards and best practices, which criminalization effectively precludes, would be helpful to both sex workers and third parties.

In short, our exploration of the administrative and security services and organizational infrastructure provided by third parties, as well as the tensions, conflicts, and resistance they occasion, highlights the impacts of criminalization on the employment relationship between sex workers and third parties in the incall/outcall sector. If criminalizing third parties has not ended this relationship, it has certainly prevented third parties from being held accountable for unfair labour practices. In this respect, the most pragmatic legal and social approach should be based on an understanding of third parties as the banal managers and administrators research shows them to be.

Notes

1 In incall establishments, clients come to the agency to receive services; outcall denotes that sex workers go to clients' homes or hotels.
2 Contractors are freelance workers paid on a fee-for-service or shift-rate basis who are hired by independent sex workers or agencies to provide specific services or clusters of services, including such things as receptionist duties, transportation, security, and web support (see also Bruckert and Law, 2013).
3 Associates are in symbiotic and mutually beneficial relationships with sex workers. They include, for example, agents, mentors, event planners, and worksite providers who *work with* sex workers (see also Bruckert and Law, 2013).
4 In legalized regimes prostitution is still perceived as problematic and, accordingly, regulated through administrative and criminal law; it is permitted only under very specific circumstances. By contrast, decriminalized regimes that foreground sex workers' human and labour

rights regulate sex work in a manner in keeping with similar occupations (e.g., occupational health and safety).

5 In New Zealand and Nevada, condom use is mandated. See Bruckert and Hannem (2013) for more on this topic.

6 Translated passage.

7 "Girlfriend experience" (for male workers it is called the "BFE" or "boyfriend experience") implies a more "emotional" or intimate experience and can involve full service, kissing, cuddling, and eating meals together. Adding to the confusion, the exact meaning of the term and what services are included vary within the sex industry.

8 Translated passage.

9 BBW, the acronym for "big beautiful woman," is commonly used in the sex industry.

10 Translated passage.

11 Moreover, in the sex industry, everyday operational tasks are more difficult to organize "because of the illegality of certain aspects of it … you can't just hire people to do one-off stuff for you" (Rhonda, workplace provider, Toronto).

12 In this context a good service would mean, for example, a clean premises (for an incall), punctuality, and the provision of the expected service for the agreed upon price.

13 Of course this is against the law in Canada. However, Rose's narrative here reminds us that such negotiations can sometimes be beneficial to sex workers.

14 Translated passage.

15 Third parties in Bowen, Bungay, and Zangger's study (2015) argued that criminalization "encouraged the involvement of people into the sex industry who were seeking to make a 'fast buck,' rather than establishing businesses that implemented safe and ethical operating policies" (40).

16 For more on the issue of wilful blindness, see Bruckert and Law, 2013.

17 See also Benoit et al., 2014 and Bowen, Bungay, and Zangger, 2015.

18 Many, but not all, agencies demand exclusivity. However, an essentially universal expectation is that sex workers do not "steal" clients by giving their contact information to customers so as to bypass the agency (and thus avoid paying them a cut) in the future.

19 It is not evident if sex workers would embrace the ability to be employees. In Germany, where the 2002 *German Prostitution Act* created the opportunity for sex workers to enter into formal contractual relationships with third parties – which would ensure they were compensated for their time waiting for clients and had access to health insurance and pensions –

few have availed themselves of the right. German sex workers report they
fear a formal record of their having worked in the sex industry, fear losing
sexual autonomy, and do not want to pay deductions (Kavemann and
Rabe, 2007).
20 Translated passage.

5 Third Parties and the Employment Relationship: The Erotic Dance Sector in Ontario

TUULIA LAW

Strip clubs occupy a legal grey area in which they are subject to municipal by-laws, and sometimes federal laws, but not provincial labour standards. Furthermore, although lap dancing is municipally prohibited (but not criminalized), it is common practice and virtually the sole source of income for dancers. As in the incall/outcall sector of the sex industry, dancers, considered by third parties to be independent contractors, are in effect dependent upon third parties to provide the location and support for their work. Drawing on interviews with third parties and dancers working in Toronto and Ottawa gathered as part of the Management Project this chapter examines this employment relationship, and with it, the work of third parties.

After a brief overview of the socio-legal context and literature, this chapter charts the roles and responsibilities of third parties who work at strip clubs, including managers, bouncers/doormen, and disc jockeys (DJs). It then examines power and resistance in relationships between dancers and third parties, as well as occupational health and safety, and, finally, the impact of municipal regulation on strip club policies and practices. Reflecting on the interplay of these themes from a labour perspective allows for a re-evaluation of stereotypical assumptions about third party control and worker agency in the sex industry. In highlighting the independent yet interdependent relationship between dancers and third parties, this chapter positions the strip club as a workplace characterized by cooperation and conflict, unfair labour practices, and creative resistance.

Erotic Dance in Ontario

The contemporary organization and regulation of stripping in Ontario are intimately connected to lap dancing, which first appeared in the 1990s. Table dancing had already transformed dancers from waged

performers to entrepreneurs who earn their income by soliciting customers for private dances; the advent of lap dancing introduced touching and doubled prices from $10 to $20 (Bruckert, 2002). By the early
2000s, clubs had virtually ceased paying dancers – only a few waged
dancers ("house girls") remained, the vast majority now considered
independent contractors (or "freelancers"). Although dancers had
already long been considered independent contractors, thanks to a
1981 Labour Board ruling declaring them ancillary to clubs' principal
income-generating activity (alcohol provision) and not economically
dependent on one employer, management began using this status to
justify charging dancers a daily ("house" or "floor") fee (Bouclin, 2009,
49–50) of $10 to $50 to access the clubs' services, facilities, and customers (Bouclin, 2004; Law, 2012).

In addition to moral outrage, bawdy house (CC s. 210) and obscene
performance charges (CC s. 167), lap dancing precipitated the development of by-laws banning touching in Toronto in 1995 and in Ottawa a
year later (Bruckert and Dufresne, 2002; Lewis, 1999). In spite of this,
lap dancing became common practice in Ontario after *R v Pelletier* found
touching not to contravene community standards of tolerance in 1999
(Bruckert and Dufresne, 2002). Although dancers have grown increasingly accustomed to lap dancing as it has become their principal source
of income, they remain somewhat divided on the matter; some, framing
it as a threat to their well-being, sexual health, and physical security,
liken it to prostitution, while others find it lucrative and feel in control
(Bouclin, 2009; Bruckert and Parent, 2007; Lewis, 2000; MLS, 2012a).
Indeed various sexual services (colloquially referred to as "extras") are
known to be offered in strip clubs (Maticka-Tyndale et al., 1999 and
2000; MLS, 2012b). Although Toronto recently refined its by-law to
apply only to certain parts of the body – including breasts and buttocks
(City of Toronto, 2012) – it nonetheless prohibits most of the touching
that typically occurs during a lap dance.

In addition to regulating the conduct of dancers and patrons, the
Toronto and Ottawa by-laws delineate the geographic spaces strip clubs
are permitted to occupy through severe zoning restrictions (see City of
Ottawa, 2004; *Toronto Municipal Code*, 2010). Furthermore, the areas of
the club in which lap dances are performed (VIP or champagne rooms)
must meet specific guidelines designed to facilitate visibility for security purposes (see City of Ottawa, 2004; City of Toronto, 2012). Municipalities also scrutinize the character of strip club workers by requiring a
police record check for all erotic entertainment licence applications (see

City of Ottawa, 2004; *Toronto Municipal Code*, 2010). Licences are obliga-tory for owners and operators in both cities. Toronto licenses dancers as well, while in Ottawa club owners are instead required to keep an annual registry listing dancers' contact information and to share this information with municipal officials upon request.

Municipal officials articulated the rationale behind these by-laws as concern for health and safety, which Bruckert and Dufresne (2002) argue derived from a discourse of morality (see also Jackson, 2011; Lewis, 1999; Machen, 1996). Worryingly, more overtly moralistic con-cerns are evident in the *Protection of Communities and Exploited Persons Act* (PCEPA) of 2014, which removed the definition of "prostitution" from the *Criminal Code*, rendering lap dancing vulnerable to increased scrutiny under the potentially far broader reach of "sexual services." Although this act came into effect after the Management Project's data collection period ended, both the literature and participants' narratives featured in this chapter suggest that moralistic regulation does not result in better health and safety outcomes.

Third Parties in the Erotic Dance Literature

Within the literature examining erotic dance, there has emerged a small body of scholarship that considers working conditions, workplace orga-nization, and third party roles and responsibilities, albeit with little data garnered from third parties directly.[1] This literature includes inquiries into surveillance and social control in erotic dance clubs (Egan, 2004; Lavin, 2013; Murphy, 2003); the regulation and organization of labour (Althorp, 2013; Barton, 2006; Bradley-Engen and Hobbs, 2010);[2] occupa-tional health and safety (Lewis and Shaver, 2006; Maticka-Tyndale et al., 1999 and 2000); and dancer resistance (Bouclin, 2004, 2006, 2009; Bruck-ert, 2002; Egan, 2006).[3] Across these studies, some scholars understand erotic dance to be inherently harmful or sexually exploitative (Couto, 2006; Fischer, 1996; Holsopple, 1998), while others view stripping as precarious, stigmatized, or marginalized labour (Colosi, 2010a and b; Fogel and Quinlan, 2011; Machen, 1996).[4]

With regard to the latter, academics argue that clubs merely classify dancers as independent contractors to avoid providing them with the benefits to which employees are entitled while simultaneously sub-jecting them to varying degrees of managerial control (Althorp, 2013; Bruckert, 2002; Couto, 2006; Fischer, 1996; Fogel and Quinlan, 2011; Price, 2008; Machen, 1996). In spite of this, scholars have observed

dancers regularly engaging in individual acts of resistance, and sometimes collective resistance as well (Althorp, 2013; Bruckert, 2002; Colosi,
2010a and b; Egan, 2004; Lavin, 2013; Lewis, 2006; Murphy, 2003).

   In terms of club operation, owners were found to be relatively uninvolved on a day-to-day basis (Lavin, 2013), unless they are also the manager (usually at a small club) (Bruckert, 2002; Price, 2008; DeMichele
and Tewksbury, 2004), whereas managers are responsible for the dancers and staff, as well as business-related considerations such as branding (Murphy, 2003; see also Bruckert, 2002). Middle-management-type
roles identified in the literature include DJs, whose authority over dancers is for the most part limited to the stage (Bruckert, 2002; Lewis, 2006;
Price-Glynn, 2010), and bouncers/doormen who are responsible for
security, collecting fees, and monitoring dancers' and patrons' conduct
(Bruckert, 2002; DeMichele and Tewksbury, 2004; Egan, 2004; Lewis,
2006; Lilleston et al., 2012). Third parties not employed by strip clubs
include companies (Price-Glynn, 2010) and agents (Althorp, 2013) for
touring dancers, as well as drivers (Bruckert, 2002).

   Academics also identified a variety of measures, as well as some serious lacunae, in strip clubs' occupational health and safety practices. Facility cleanliness and safety measures were more often found to be lacking
(see Althorp, 2013; Bruckert, Parent, and Robitaille, 2003; Couto, 2006;
Price-Glynn, 2010) than adequate (see Colosi, 2010a; Lilleston et al., 2012).
Furthermore, scholars noted that house rules and the surveillance of
dancer-client interactions by third parties is a largely ineffective measure
against sexual harassment, assault, or the provision of sexual services.[5]

Sample

Although this chapter builds on some issues addressed in the literature,
in talking with third parties directly the Management Project marks
an important contribution to empirical knowledge about strip club
management in Ontario. To this end, this chapter draws on individual
interviews with 13 third parties and 2 focus groups with a total of 8
dancers. All participants had experience working in the erotic dance sector
in Ontario[6] as of the year 2000. All of the 13 strip industry third parties
interviewed were men, with careers in the erotic dance sector spanning
from 6 months to 22 years. Most work (or had worked) at mainstream
female strip clubs save for 2 (these participants were also the only ones
with experience as sex workers). As to their particular occupations, 3
work(ed) as managers, 2 as DJs, 4 as managers/DJs (or some combination

thereof[7]), one as a bouncer, 3 as bouncer/managers, and one as a driver and protection provider. Our sample of third parties was predominantly white, with only 2 racialized men, both of whom identified as Black. Seven of these men work or had worked in Toronto, and the remaining 6 in Ottawa. Our focus-group participants were all white women who had spent 5 to 19 years working in the industry. Because some dancers had experience in both Ottawa and Toronto, in the coming pages dancers are classified by focus group rather than the city or cities where they work(ed).

Third Party Roles, Practices, and Responsibilities

Recalling that third parties are individuals who organize, supervise, facilitate, or coordinate the labour of sex workers, all of the erotic dance sector third parties interviewed for this study can be described as having one or several of these elements as part of their particular occupation, which they in turn balance with their specific contributions to the operation of the club. Whereas managers are responsible for the bar as a whole, and as such are imbued with broad "formal" authority (Bruckert, 2002), other third party roles nonetheless entail various (comparatively more narrow) supervisory capacities over dancers. The division of labour among third parties varies from club to club; like mainstream organizations, individual roles become more specialized in larger clubs and more multifaceted in smaller ones (Daft and Armstrong, 2009). For example, at some clubs DJs collect floor fees from dancers and sign them in when they arrive, whereas at other establishments bouncers take care of these tasks. Adam (manager and DJ, Toronto) told us that at one club where he had worked, DJs organize dancers' work schedules, whereas Reverend (Ottawa) sometimes helps with this as the head doorman/manager. At some clubs, bouncers also hire dancers and/or other bouncers. Other duties, such as monitoring customers' and dancers' behaviour, are shared among bouncers, managers, and DJs.

As noted in several studies (Bruckert, 2002; Lavin, 2013; Murphy, 2003; Price, 2008), managers oversee the daily operation of the strip club. To this end managers "supervise everybody. You always got your eye on the bartender, the wait staff, even the cook, if there's a kitchen" (Adam, manager and DJ, Toronto). Managers' specific responsibilities, which can be categorized as supervisory and business related (see also Bruckert, 2002; Murphy, 2003), include hiring,[8] scheduling, disciplining, and firing staff and dancers; branding, advertising, and marketing; customer relations; ordering supplies (e.g., liquor); salary distribution and, some-times, accounting. Because many daily tasks are, in turn, carried out by the staff, Gilles (manager, Toronto) identified maintaining "harmony ... between staff" as key to his role as a manager. Similarly, Dalton (man-ager, Toronto) made sure his club ran smoothly by "travelling around [the club] ... not just making sure that my staff is doing their job, but also watching for hot spots." As we will see throughout this chapter, manag-ers' work permeates many aspects of the strip club: they direct staff, set and/or enforce policies and procedures, and are responsible for making sure the club follows municipal (e.g., strip club by-laws), provincial (e.g., alcohol regulation), and federal (e.g., prostitution) laws.

Unsurprisingly, DJs' primary role is to organize and announce the stage entertainment, a job in which they take pride and to which they carefully add "some kind of a personal touch ... without sounding too cliché" (Chico, DJ, Ottawa). Practically speaking, as Ottawa DJ Fuzzy Pickle points out, DJs "schedule when each girl goes on stage, right. For the most part I do it chronologically from the time that they come in ... If I find that, you know, the girls have a similar frame and hair colour, I won't put them together – or similar names." Because they organize the shows DJs interact frequently with dancers, which makes some feel like "more of a counselor sometimes" (Fuzzy Pickle, Ottawa), or a "babysitter" (Adam, Toronto; Chico, Ottawa). Although Bruckert (2002), Lewis (2006), and Price-Glynn (2010) described similarly patron-izing attitudes, in our study DJs were also found to provide organiza-tional resources to dancers. These include communicating stage show requirements – "don't be late for stage, stay up there for three minutes a song, get naked" (Studley, DJ/manager, Ottawa); offering emotional support, which Dalton (DJ and manager, Toronto) described as "be[ing] positive for the girls, and be[ing] positive about the work that they're doing"; and suggesting and/or editing songs for dancers. Such initia-tives are, in part, financially motivated. As Fuzzy Pickle explained, "if I can put a smile on their face before they leave the DJ booth, chances are they're going to do better with the customers; they're going to make more money, and I will see the results in tips at the end of the night." In this respect DJs inhabit a contradictory position insofar as they must enforce rules regarding stage shows and music (which we will exam-ine in greater detail shortly) while also relying on dancers for tips to supplement their income (see also Bruckert, 2002).

Whereas DJs engage with customers only indirectly, through the microphone and by watching from the DJ booth to see if they act inappropriately towards dancers on stage, bouncers are much more directly involved with club customers, whose behaviour forms an important part of their security mandate. In George's (Toronto) words, as a bouncer, "you're doing ID checks, making sure that guys that are sitting in pervert's row aren't going onstage, [or] grabbing the dancers, [or] putting their beers on the stage, making sure no fights break out, no one's bringing their own alcohol in." Their job may include some managerial responsibilities (as noted above), as well as "odd jobs" (see also DeMichele and Tewksbury, 2004). According to Scott (doorman and manager, Ottawa), "your boss tells you to do something, you do it." However, bouncers focus primarily on surveillance, screening, and, if necessary, enforcement. In terms of surveillance, "it's just basically making sure that everything is always operating within a legal limit … Most of it is observation – observing the customers, observing the girls" (Reverend, head doorman/manager, Ottawa). A conspicuous presence in the club, bouncers also serve as deterrence (see Bruckert, 2002; DeMichele and Tewksbury, 2004): "There's always three or four people in security and they have 'security' written on their sweaters … And they move around quite a bit," says Tony (manager/DJ, Ottawa). As in DeMichele and Tewksbury's (2004) study, bouncers are discouraged from excessive use of force; George (bouncer, Toronto) explained, "we try to talk to the customer as much as possible … [but] if there's a physical problem, majority of the time, we do have to use physical force." To this end bouncers are encouraged to pre-empt conflicts and screen out difficult customers.

Protection and the "Pimp"

Some screening policies at strip clubs appear to operate according to a broad framing of risk – for example, Adam (manager and DJ, Toronto) instructed his doormen not to admit "anybody who looks strange" – however other approaches amount to racial profiling. Although screening of young Black men is not unique to strip clubs (Koskela, 2012; Lilleston et al., 2012), it certainly appears to be prevalent in them. For example Studley (DJ/manager) informed us that at the club where he works in Ottawa, management is particularly attentive to certain attributes and behaviours that they associate with "pimps": "Black guys, none of them want a drink, none of them want to pay cover, 'Oh, I'm just waiting to talk to so-and-so,' or whatever, then every girl that walks by, they're calling them over." Indeed the majority of third parties who worked at female strip clubs espoused a particular suspicion of Black men and/or drivers, offering largely unsubstantiated or unverifiable impressions informed by popular scripts of dangerous, manipulative "pimps" (see Benson, 2012):

> I mean when you see a forty-year-old Black guy pull up in a Bentley, you know, and a twenty-year-old girl get out, and no money exchanges hands, no kisses on the cheek, no, "Bye, baby. See you later," you know, my first impulse of course would be to think that it was a driver. But again, if you don't see any money change hands, then you've got to wonder, you know. (Studley, DJ/manager, Ottawa)

This imagery of race and risk also informs other club policies that complement screening; taken together, they construct an environment that appeals to some customers at the same time as it excludes others. DJs described club rules governing dancers' music, which for the most part do not allow rap (Bruckert and Chabot 2010; Reed 1997), ostensibly because it "just doesn't fly, especially with the clientele that we have ... mid-forties to early fifties, mostly white guys" (Studley, DJ/manager, Ottawa). Although he doubted their effectiveness, Fuzzy Pickle (DJ, Ottawa) offered an explanation of the rationale underlying this and other policies: "The club is trying to do what they can to eliminate [the presence of "pimps"] as far as, you know, there's not hats allowed in the club ... No rap in the music." Informed by similar assumptions, dancers also described strategies for managing men they suspected were "pimps": some avoided Black customers altogether whereas others abandoned conversations when men in the club offered to help manage their work and/or finances. Scott (bouncer and manager, Ottawa) highlighted some of the difficulties inherent to customer profiling: "The problem was we had to be able to prove they were a pimp; 'No, no, I'm her boyfriend, I'm a regular customer, I just know her.' It became difficult." However this appears not to have discouraged third parties and dancers from screening practices based on, and perpetuating, the racial stereotype addressed throughout this collection and which, as we saw in Chapter 1 ("The Representation of the 'Pimp' ") inform media representations.

As a Black man who provided driving and protection services to a dancer, Eric (Toronto) is someone who is likely to be profiled as a "pimp" through the screening practices described above. The only third party we encountered who was not employed by a strip club, Eric described his responsibilities as follows: "Anytime she wanted to go to work ... I would drive her, and I would look out for her. And I would sit in the club and I would watch certain things; she'd always ask me to, like, not let certain guys go talk to her, or to show certain guys that I am there so that they wouldn't." In an ambiguous financial arrangement, Eric also provided money-management services to the dancer with whom he worked: "She'd make, like, five, six bills certain nights, and I wouldn't ask her for anything, but at the end of the night she'd give me two bills." Because Eric appears to have worked *with* a dancer in a symbiotic affiliation (unlike club management, which as we will see, imposes employee-like obligations on dancers), this relationship somewhat resembles an "associate" relationship (see Introduction; Bruckert and Law, 2013).

Workplace Relationships, Power, and Resistance

With the exception of the driver and the housemother,[9] whose direct fee-for-supplies/service arrangements more closely resemble "contractor" relationships (outlined in the Introduction), dancers' relationships with strip club third parties are shaped by the contradictions of the so-called independent contractor relationship. In this arrangement dancers govern their own entrepreneurial interactions with customers, in which third parties are largely uninvolved. Third parties do, however, organize and (through hiring and firing) control dancers' access to supports essential to their income – the club, its customers and amenities (e.g., security, music, bar service, VIP rooms, etc.) – through which they incentivize dancers to provide quality service to customers and regulate their behaviour. In turn, it is in dancers' interest to give quality customer service, since poor service would hinder their personal business, as well as the club's success, which is required for continued employment by third parties. In this respect, dancers and third parties are both interdependent on, and independent of, each other. Scott (bouncer and manager, Ottawa) offered the following reflection on this disruption of traditional organizational hierarchy:

> Some of the managers and doormen are of the state of mind that these girls work for us. They don't work with us. They're not fellow staff members. They come in, they make this bar money and then they go ... So that whole with and for slash gets a little blurry when it comes to the dancers ... I mean, my job was to regulate them. But, without them, I'm not

making money. So in that sense, I kind of see them, you know, kind of almost equal. I [only] have a little bit authority over them.

In order to manage the conflicts engendered by this employment relationship (e.g., abuse of authority), dancers engage with third parties instrumentally, manipulatively, or with various forms of resistance, which we will examine in the next section.

Third parties' aesthetic expectations significantly impact dancers, who told us that women are often fired for being "overweight" or "too old." In keeping with the findings of Maticka-Tyndale (2004), Price-Glynn (2010), and Bruckert and Frigon (2003), hiring criteria largely reflect Western ideals of female beauty (i.e., slim, young, and white). Some of our respondents, especially Dalton (DJ and manager, Toronto), struggled with enforcing these criteria:

> If you're Black and heavy, you're certainly not getting in. If you're Black, you may get in, but you better be real good looking, you know. And you better be not an instigator, right. And yes ... that was a real contradiction for me, you know, being Black and having to tell Black women, "No, you can't work here" ... Very, very difficult.

Disturbingly, with the exception of the club where Charlene (Toronto focus group) dances, all of the female strip clubs in our sample had a racial quota of three to five Black dancers per shift. In the words of Fuzzy Pickle (DJ, Ottawa),

> There's quite a bit of discrimination ... On any given night, I can have as many white girls as you can throw at me; I'm only allowed to have five Black girls ... They're trying to limit the amount of pimps they let into the club, and they – I guess the thought is that Black girls will bring in the Black guys that are, obviously, the pimps.

Thus racial quotas appear to be informed by racist perceptions, through which Black women are framed as both risky, based on their presumed association with "dangerous" Black men (Brooks, 2010), and undesirable, based on the normative assumptions about clients' preferences: "The customers wanted usually the stereotypical white blonde big-breasted bimbo or other variety of girls – Asian girls, brunette girls, redhead girls, uh, but only so many Blacks" (Scott, bouncer and manager, Ottawa). Racial quotas inform not only who is allowed to work, but also when they can work: at Fuzzy Pickle's (DJ, Ottawa) club "they literally will only schedule five, and if a sixth comes in and wants to freelance, she's sent home because there's too many Black girls."[10]

Although racial quotas appear to be quite consistent in Ottawa and Toronto, other scheduling policies differ significantly between the two cities. In Ottawa, for example,

[dancers] have a minimum that they have to complete one of the quieter shifts during the week ... And they can work any other days that they want. I will ask girls to work ... a minimum of three [shifts] ... But if you're not here on the day that you're scheduled, I'm going to be looking for you, and there could be consequences for not showing up for your shift – especially if you don't call. (Reverend, head doorman/manager)

In short, Ottawa clubs require dancers to perform unpaid labour (stage shows and being present for a fixed number of hours) in exchange for access to the club. By contrast, in Toronto scheduled dancers are compensated at something approximating minimum wage but are significantly outnumbered by independent contractors ("freelancers"). Clubs' unwillingness to increase their roster of waged dancers means that in some ways the dancer labour force is largely out of their control. Adam (manager and DJ) explained the consequences of this staffing model:

It's a chicken-and-egg thing. If you have girls, you have customers. If you don't have customers, you don't have girls ... So there are some days where you have a lot of girls and you don't have enough customers to service the girls ... in which case then you've got a lot of bitter women who think, "Oh, well, this is going to be a shitty week." And then, they take the next day off. And then, the next day rolls around and there are a lot of customers and there aren't enough girls. And then, the customers leave because there's not enough girls to service the customers. There's no way to fix it. There's nothing you can do. You can promote the bar all you like, you can hire as many dancers as you want, but who shows up on a day-to-day basis is completely random.

The unreliability of a predominantly freelance workforce, in turn, creates leeway for scheduled dancers to resist managerial expectations during unpopular (i.e., afternoon) shifts: "You could be, like, twenty minutes or half an hour late, and it didn't really matter," explained Sasha (Ottawa focus group).

Acknowledging the DJ's significant authority over her labour as a scheduled dancer, Sasha "would call the DJ because I liked the DJ, and I thought it was important to get along with him." DJs' authority varies according to how often dancers are required to perform on stage, a matter in which freelancers (in Toronto) have some choice: "When you're new, you usually have to go on stage, and after you've been there for a while, you don't have to go so much" (Carrie, Toronto focus group). By contrast, maintaining a good relationship with managers seems less important to some. Like Sasha, Donna (Ottawa focus group) "just wanted them [managers] to leave me alone and not bother me." However, Bobby (Toronto focus group) thought it imperative to get along with the third party responsible for organizing her schedule. Dancers' perception of the importance of their relationships with third parties, in turn, influences how they interact with them.

Dancer Resistance: Limits and Strategies

While some dancers make a conscious decision to appear compliant – "I don't want to risk getting fired, so I'm just not going to speak up" (Donna, Ottawa focus group) – others resist third parties or engage with them strategically. Brigitte, Carrie, Donna, and Leigh (Toronto focus group) agreed that flirting and subtle manipulation were more effective than projecting a professional attitude in order to get third parties to capitulate to their demands (see also Bruckert, 2002; Colosi, 2010b). However Brigitte told us she "would feel like if I didn't flirt back with them that, like, it would cause problems." Recognizing the effectiveness of these gendered manipulation tactics but not wanting to engage in them herself, Charlene (Toronto focus group) approached third parties instrumentally, "ask[ing] them all sorts of personal questions about themselves so that, that way, they don't see me as a dancer who constantly, chronically complains ... They're always willing to help me out because I'm always interested in what they're doing as people."

When flirtatiousness turns to brazen abuse of power and sexual harassment, dancers may mobilize strategies of resistance. For example, Sasha (Ottawa focus group) rebuffed a manager who "tried to touch me while he was giving me the shift pay" one too many times by telling him " 'this is not a lap dance.' And he was like, 'Okay.' " A similar moment of resistance by Jen (Toronto focus group), who along with a friend got propositioned by a club owner, elicited a rather different response: "We were like, 'Oh, no. You know, thank you for the offer' ... And we got fired." As we saw in the previous chapter on incall/outcall workers, without access to labour complaints mechanisms, dancers must resolve workplace issues by drawing on their courage and creativity to enact strategies that may, in the end, nonetheless result in termination.

As other scholars have observed, although dancers engaged in individual acts of resistance, they seldom resisted collectively or tried to enact structural change in the workplace (Althorp, 2013; Bouclin, 2004; Bruckert, 2002; Colosi, 2010a; Egan, 2004). Donna (Ottawa focus group) recounted one such situation:

> I did step up, and I attempted to get collective action, and it totally failed
> … They [her colleagues] weren't interested. They were just too scared of
> getting fired and losing their job. And I do know that managers in Ottawa
> will call other managers and report someone as a troublemaker.

Indeed Tony (manager/DJ, Ottawa) told us about getting just such a call. Bouclin (2004 and 2009) similarly found that managers in Ottawa cooperated to "blacklist" dancers known to be labour agitators. Likewise, Leigh's (Toronto focus group) requests for change-room maintenance at a staff meeting were also met with hostility from management (see also Althorp, 2013; Price-Glynn, 2010): "I'd be dismissed, like, 'I didn't come here for that. This is the end of this meeting.' And then [the manager would] leave." However, Sasha (Ottawa focus group) told us about dancers successfully resisting management's sudden imposition of a 10 per cent cut of their cash earnings. In contrast to Egan's (2004) study, in which dancers resisted paying the cut on an ongoing individual basis, this was a collective act of passive noncompliance: as Sasha explained, the dancers "just kind of complained about it to each other, and then … everyone just stopped cooperating, and then the managers never talked about it again."

Third Party Resistance, Relating, and Opportunism

Like managerial actors below the ownership level of any organization, strip club third parties can be seen simultaneously as exploitative agents of capital and subjugated workers (Willmott, 1997). From this contradictory and precarious position (Willmott, 1997) they may not have the authority or capacity to adequately attend to workers' needs, health, and safety (Bolton and Houlihan, 2010). In response, third parties sometimes misbehave or resist organizational goals and rules (Young, 2000).

As with dancers, third parties may resist by withholding their labour because they feel undercompensated by the club – unsurprisingly this is more often the case with DJs and bouncers than with managers, who enjoy more authority and higher wages. This may, in turn, have a negative effect on dancers (even though it is of course the club owner, not dancers, who sets third parties' wages). For example, George (bouncer, Toronto) recalled that "when there's payment issues ... you try your hardest to get the girl the money. And even then the girls treat us like assholes ... They don't care ... So it's hard to go out of your way the next time."

Third parties also resist relations of power in the strip club in their own financial or other personal interests, which Bruckert (2002, 43) refers to as the "informal economy of favours." For example, Fuzzy Pickle (DJ, Ottawa) took advantage of a manager's absence by canceling a nightly promotional event that the dancers did not like: "It wasn't that busy, and I didn't want to interrupt the girls that were making some money to bring them out to do a free dance because at the end of the day, the more money the girls make, the better my night is going to be ... So I just skipped over it." Other DJs are motivated by tips to accommodate dancers who want to postpose their stage show in order to spend more time with a customer. Similarly bouncers and (less often) managers may endeavour to earn tips by matching dancers with clients: "[Customers] would say, 'I'm looking for this ... kind of girl ... I go find the girl. I hook the girls up with the client. The girl might give me a tip if they make a lot of money ... That was an opportunity to make money that I saw that I jumped on" (Scott, bouncer and manager, Ottawa).

As we will see later in this chapter, third party resistance to club rules or other third parties often overlaps with resistance to the state (e.g., laws or by-laws). Sometimes, however, this resistance coalesces with opportunism, resulting in tactics that undermine dancers' safety and/ or financial interests:

> We've even had doormen ... who would try to extort from girls, whether it be financial or sexual ... Basically, you catch a girl in a position where she's already breaking the rules to the point where she'd probably just get fired on the spot, but instead, it's like, "Oh, I'll let this go if" – I don't know – "you sleep with me or you pay me or both." (Reverend, head doorman/ manager)

Risk Management and Occupational Health and Safety

The opportunism of the economy of favours may in turn affect dancers' safety and security: for example, Donna (Ottawa focus group) was of the opinion that "the only time a bouncer would really do anything for me was if I tipped him." In addition, since bouncers and (perhaps especially) managers must juggle multiple responsibilities spread over different areas of the club, they may not be nearby when dancers are experiencing difficulties with customers. As a result, some managers offer advice to dancers on how to mitigate risks themselves. For example, Adam (manager and DJ, Toronto) instructed dancers to "pick and choose your battles, right? Like, pick, pick a customer. If a customer seems creepy to you, he is probably creepy. You know, if you don't want to get ripped off, collect your money more often." Dalton (DJ and manager, Toronto) warned dancers against getting too drunk for similar reasons: "This is not the kind of image you want to present of yourself. Think about it ... only the bad guys want the, you know, the heavy drunk girls. They got bad intentions." This kind of safety advice, though intended as a preventative measure, effectively offloads responsibility for risk management onto dancers.

Although bouncers (and to a lesser extent, managers) are responsible for intervening when a customer causes harm, dancers told us third parties do not always take transgressions seriously. For example, after a customer had sexually assaulted her, Brigitte (Toronto focus group) "asked [the manager] if he could please ask that guy to leave because I didn't want it to happen to another girl, and he said 'no.' " This is not always the case. Scott (Ottawa) insisted that, "as a doorman, there have been many times when I've gotten physically involved violently, uh, to keep the girls safe." Nonetheless, in response to what some perceived as a lack of interest in their well-being, as well as an acknowledgement that third parties are not always available, dancers felt it necessary to be prepared to resolve their own issues with customers. As Carrie (Toronto focus group) said, "you have to be tough."[11]

Similarly it appears that third parties care about dancers' financial well-being to varying extents. Leigh (Toronto focus group) described managers defending her interests in disputes with customers, while Donna (Ottawa focus group) and Bobby (Toronto focus group) had found them unhelpful. Brigitte, Carrie (Toronto focus group), and Sasha (Ottawa focus group) had all worked at a club where management refunds dancers up to one hundred dollars in house-fee credits if a customer refuses to pay. At the club where George (bouncer) works, doormen endeavour to prevent financial disputes with customers by "record[ing] the girls' times when they come up [to VIP]. You put their name and their time ... The songs run for four minutes, so we keep track ... that way." Third parties also sometimes involve the police when financial disputes arise, however, as Reverend (head doorman/ manager, Ottawa) pointed out, "by law, they have to pay, but ... it's hard to prove everything."

In addition to risks from customers, dancers face health and safety hazards emanating from the condition and maintenance of the club itself. Fuzzy Pickle (DJ, Ottawa), Scott (bouncer and manager, Ottawa), and Studley (DJ and manager, Ottawa) told us they were vigilant about promptly cleaning up liquids or broken glass to prevent dancers from getting injured. Although Sasha and Donna (Ottawa focus group) found this to be true, other dancers claimed that neither the pole nor the stage were regularly cleaned. Indeed, for the most part dancers reported disinterest and neglect towards facilities on the part of third parties (see also Althorp, 2013). Problems included inadequate and/or unsanitary staff bathrooms and change rooms; holes in the floor underneath the carpeting; furniture in the change rooms; and VIP rooms in poor condition. Such neglect heightens dancers' physical health risks: Carrie and Leigh (Toronto focus group), for example, had gotten rashes at work, while others worried about falling on a slippery stage or an uneven floor. Unfortunately, because dancers are independent contractors, they are exempt from the labour protections afforded to employees, including provincial occupational health and safety regulations and complaints mechanisms (Lewis and Shaver, 2006). Although by-laws in Toronto and Ottawa mandate adequate and clean workspaces and staff washrooms (see City of Ottawa, 2004; *Toronto Municipal Code*, 2010), the problematic conditions described by dancers suggests there is little interest among municipal agents in enforcing them.

Regulation and Rules

Just as health and labour standards in strip clubs are woefully under-regulated (as we have seen in the prevalence of workplace hazards and hiring discrimination, especially through the enforcement of racial "quotas"),[12] municipal by-laws over-regulate conduct perceived to be sexually risky or morally questionable (Bruckert, Parent, and Robitaille,

2003; Bruckert and Dufresne, 2002). This results in surveillance of the club and its workers by agents of the state, and also informs club rules and practices.

Although Adam (manager and DJ, Toronto) and Chico (DJ, Ottawa) suggested that police raids declined over the years as lap dancing became increasingly institutionalized, participants told us about routine (though not necessarily frequent) by-law inspections, in which officers "just give us attitude" (George, bouncer, Toronto). Indeed, it appears by-law officers in Toronto are chiefly concerned with inspecting dancers' licences. Considered alongside the lack of attention to facilities noted above, we see that, while the by-laws provide for an additional level of state surveillance, in effect they do not result in useful oversight of dancers' health or safety.

Nor do by-laws function as consistent guidelines for workplace practices. Noting a discrepancy between what the by-laws say and what municipal inspectors actually enforce (see for example, *City of Toronto v. Zanzibar, 2007*), Adam was of the opinion that "it's like they've basically given up on the by-law that still stands that says there's not supposed to be any contact ... And it's a just very grey area that makes it difficult to ... police what goes on in your club." Accordingly, house rules about what constitutes an appropriate level (and nature) of touching vary by club. For Dalton (manager, Toronto), the limit was "nobody ejaculates in my club." By contrast, the rules at Tony's (manager/DJ, Ottawa) club are more specific: "No grinding, no, you know, sexual activities ... But if the girls allow a customer to touch their buttocks or their boobs, that's up to them." As Sasha (Ottawa focus group) recounted, some clubs – like incall and outcall establishments – attempt to mitigate the risks of nebulous regulations by offloading legal liability onto dancers (cf. Chapkis, 2000; Egan, 2004; Lewis, 1999): "I had to sign this paper at the beginning basically saying, like, I wouldn't do lap dances ... They [management] kind of said, like, 'this is to, you know, avoid by-law difficulties.' "

However, as dancers and third parties were equally aware, touching and sexual services occur in spite of by-laws and house rules. In this respect the enforcement of these rules and regulations varies as well. Some clubs implement rather strict regulations. For example, at Tony's (manager/DJ, Ottawa) club, "if the girls are found to be doing sexual activities they will be escorted out of the premises immediately." At Studley's club in Ottawa, anxiety about unsanctioned services manifests in oversight of dancers' break time: "[dancers] can't leave the club for more than fifteen minutes at a time ... because we're worried girls might be turning tricks in the parking lot." Here we see that third parties' surveillance of dancers is also informed by federal criminal laws pertaining to prostitution; that said, the by-laws appear to be a higher priority, given the sanctioned activity that routinely occurs during lap dances, the monitoring of which would pre-empt any prostitution-like activities. Dex (manager, Toronto) explained his rationale for heavy surveillance: "It's a lot more profitable to maintain a clean bar, with dancers who are only dancing and giving lap dances that adhere to the law." As Donna (Ottawa focus group) explained, however, managerial attempts at enforcing the by-laws can result in "rather ridiculous rules. Like, they had one rule that you ... always had to have one foot on the floor ... even if I was sitting next to my customer and just wanted to have a drink and put my feet up because they hurt." In this context, bouncers "touring the champagne rooms to make sure we were safe ... felt more like they were supervising me" (Donna).

The more common approach seems to be wilful blindness, by which third parties merely aim to, in the words of Dalton (manager, Toronto), "put a front on that you are following all the rules." This manifests as an "if we don't see it happening, it's not happening kind of mentality ... [but] if we catch you doing it, then you're in trouble" (Studley, DJ/manager, Ottawa).[13] Indeed, it appears as though wilful blindness is not just a practice used by some third parties but a policy at certain clubs. For example, Troy (manager, Toronto) and his fellow managers "didn't go back in the [VIP] booths ... because it was our choice not to police." Whether they manifest as infrequent rounds through VIP or wilful blindness outright, such policies can be confusing to third parties below the managerial level, as George (bouncer, Toronto) explained: "They tell me they don't want the extras going on. They say to report it. I have reported it. I've gotten in more trouble than the dancers. So to me, it's, what's the point of the reporting?"

As Adam (manager and DJ, Toronto) explained, too much surveillance of dancers' interactions with customers can be bad for business: "If you've got a bouncer wandering around and poking his head in the booths every five seconds to make sure something not right is happening, you've ruined it for the client, who's paying good money to enjoy, you know, a dance." Similarly Donna (Ottawa focus group) said that, "to have a bouncer coming in the champagne room literally every song was very distracting to them [her customers] ... It impacted my business." In their mutual agreement that the by-laws can hinder customer satisfaction, we see an instance in which dancers' and third parties' interests overlap and are interdependent. The prevalence of wilful blindness, then, speaks to the economic importance of lap dancing. Moreover, that it is common practice in spite of the stipulation in the by-laws that third parties are responsible for the services dancers offer suggests that the 2014 PCEPA may have similar effects if applied to strip clubs.

As with the incall/outcall agencies discussed in Chapter 4, wilful blindness can have negative ramifications on dancers' health and safety. Adam (manager and DJ, Toronto) expressed concern about dancers' sexual health in this regard:

> You would hope that if someone was practising sex in the strip club ... that they would practise safe sex. But that's not really something you can police ... You can't sort of go around [and] say, "Well, if you're going to do it, make sure you do it safely." Because that would imply that you accept the fact that it's happening when it's not supposed to be happening.

With her fellow Toronto focus group participants nodding in agreement (but see MLS, 2012a), Leigh told us she was primarily concerned about the impact of wilful blindness on her safety: "I wish that they would cross out a lot of these archaic laws because I feel more safe having everything allowed so that the staff is not afraid to protect us." In other words, removing the sanctions against sexual touching would remove the need for wilful blindness, enabling third parties to protect dancers' safety and financial interests even if they choose to allow customers to touch them or agree to offer "extras."

Concluding Reflections

In this chapter we have seen that strip club third parties' relationships with, and authority over, dancers vary with their roles and responsibilities. Whereas managers' administrative duties in regard to dancers are, by their nature, periodic (e.g., hiring, disciplining, firing, scheduling) or at arm's length (e.g., oversight of club operation), bouncers occupy more of a surveillance/ disciplinary role (monitoring dancers' interactions with clients to ensure safety, legality, and payment), while DJs organize dancers' labour on a daily basis (managing the only aspect of dancers' work done explicitly for the benefit of the club – the stage show). We have also considered third parties who operate outside of the organizational structure of the club – drivers and "pimps" – whose roles and relationships with dancers are read through racial and class scripts of dangerousness (see Benson, 2012).

We have also seen how the independent contractor relationship challenges conventional notions of workplace hierarchy insofar as third parties and dancers are mutually dependent on customers, whom they both aim to satisfy through the environment of the club and the quality of its services. At the same time they are independent of each other in the performance of their particular roles. In addition to providing dancers with leeway to organize how (and in Toronto, when) they work, the independent contractor relationship allows dancers to form individual working relationships with third parties – for example, with DJs or bouncers – through the "informal economy of favours" (Bruckert, 2002, 43). Although dancers are limited by managerial expectations and rules, in addition to the infeasibility of unionization (see Couto, 2006), their resistance strategies demonstrate that they are creative and savvy in navigating problematic workplace and employment conditions. The necessity of these strategies also highlights how existing regulations focusing on sexual conduct are confusing, poorly communicated, unevenly applied, and ultimately ineffective in protecting dancers' safety and well-being. A more consistent and efficient approach to workplace safety would be to regulate and monitor facility maintenance and support labour rights. Unfortunately, dancers share in the challenges faced by the growing segment of workers in Canada's labour market who inhabit a similarly interdependent yet independent relationship with their employers, "making out" (Burawoy, 1979) amidst a dearth of mechanisms to defend their rights, health, and safety (see Fudge et al., 2003).

Notes

1 However, some studies include interviews with third parties as a secondary focus. See for example Barton, 2006; Bruckert, 2002; Colosi, 2010a and 2010b; Egan, 2004; Lavin, 2013; Lewis, 2006; Lilleston et al., 2012; Murphy, 2003; Price, 2008; and Price-Glynn, 2010). Only DeMichele and Tewksbury (2004) focus primarily on third parties (bouncers). Only Bruckert (2002) and Lewis (2006) conducted their studies in Ontario.
2 See also Bruckert, 2002; Bruckert, Parent, and Robitaille, 2003; Colosi, 2010a and 2010b; Lewis, 2006; Machen, 1996; Price, 2008; and Price-Glynn, 2010.
3 See also Lilleston et al., 2012; and Maticka-Tyndale, 2004.
4 See also Bouclin, 2004, 2006, 2009; Bruckert, 2002; Bruckert et al., 2003;

DeMichele and Tewksbury, 2004; Egan, 2006; Lavin, 2013; Lewis and Shaver, 2006; and Maticka-Tyndale, 2004.

5 For more on this topic see Egan, 2006; DeMichele and Tewksbury, 2004; Lavin, 2013; Lewis, 2006; Lewis and Shaver, 2006; Lilleston et al., 2012; Maticka-Tyndale, 2004; Maticka-Tyndale et al., 1999, 2000; MLS, 2012a; Murphy, 2003; and Price, 2008.

6 Unlike the other chapters, this chapter pertains only to the work of third parties and dancers in Ontario.

7 Some of these men had managed and DJ'd as separate positions, whereas for others, these roles were combined in the same job. As such, the title "manager and DJ" refers to the former and is distinct from "manager/DJ," which refers to the latter. Readers will note such distinctions for doormen as well.

8 Although it appears no training is offered to dancers, managers provide a cursory explanation of house rules and policies to new hires.

9 The housemother identified by dancers in this research did not quite fit our operationalization of a third party. Leigh (Toronto focus group) contrasted the housemothers she had worked with in the United States (see Murphy, 2003; Price, 2008; Price-Glynn, 2010), who acted more as "supervisors … somebody you can go to instead of the manager," to her Ontario equivalent, who is "more of a cleaning lady" who, as Charlene (Toronto focus group) claimed, provides dancers with "sundries."

10 This practice appears to be longstanding in Ontario (see Bouclin, 2004; Bruckert and Frigon, 2003) and common across the erotic dance sector. For example Brooks (2010, 1997; see also Price-Glynn, 2010) has noted scheduling practices in strip clubs in the United States that award the most lucrative shifts to white, conventionally attractive dancers.

11 For more information on dancers' security strategies, see Law, 2016.

12 A dearth of labour-standards enforcement, or perhaps a lack of interest in examining adherence to labour rights, visible in the ease with which strip clubs exclude dancers whom they deem to be unsuitable for clients' preferences (i.e., Black, fat, tattooed, or visibly pregnant women), may also facilitate the lack of gender parity in third party roles in Ontario's erotic dance sector. This speculation arises from the fact that all of the strip club third parties who participated in this research were men, and from participants' accounts suggesting that virtually all strip club third parties are men (save for a few notable exceptions of female owners or managers).

13 Third parties' attitudes towards illicit drug consumption were similar, resembling what Lavin (2013, 362) called "the path of least resistance" (see also Chapkis, 2000; DeMichele and Tewksbury, 2004; Lavin, 2013; Maticka-

Tyndale, 2004). Adam (manager and DJ, Toronto) best summarized respondents' resigned attitude to drug use: "the dancers do drugs, the staff do drugs. Um, it's just a business that caters to that sort of thing … And you just deal with it … So, if you're going to do it, try to be discreet about it."

6 Managing Sex Work: Bringing the Industry in from the Cold

LESLIE ANN JEFFREY

As we have seen throughout this collection, for many years in Canada laws and policies have associated sex industry management with "pimping" and treated it as an unalloyed evil. The research presented here, however, makes it clear that for many sex workers, as is the case for workers in other industries, being managed can provide a number of benefits. For policymakers it is therefore critical to distinguish between the problem of "being managed" and "bad management." While there may be bad management practices, this does not undermine the fact that working in a managed environment, where someone else takes responsibility for arrangements, bookings, advertising, security, set up, and so on, is a rational choice for many sex workers. Indeed it is difficult to envision how erotic dancers, for example, could undertake their labour without third party involvement (Law, this collection). Policies must therefore be directed at encouraging good management practices and weeding out bad ones, rather than suppressing management altogether. The attempt to eradicate management has clearly failed to eliminate management in the sex industry, but it has made it more difficult for good management practices to emerge fully. There are ways, however, in which the policy environment can be made conducive to good management practices in the sex industry. In this chapter we examine how certain policies and practices around sex work management – most importantly, spatial controls and labour regulations – have worked in other countries, and we draw lessons for the Canadian case.

An important fact to keep in mind while discussing policies around the sex industry is that while different forms of sex work share many characteristics with other employment fields such as other personal-care services, sex work has its own unique features, particularly the amount of stigma attached to the occupation. Stigma makes bringing sex work out "into the light" of regulation and normalization both difficult for management and sometimes dangerous for workers themselves; current federal laws and municipal by-laws surrounding sex businesses in Canada, for example, have numerous negative effects on workers and managers (see this collection; Bruckert and Law, 2013). Stigma is one of the biggest barriers to providing safe working conditions for sex workers, and while criminalization ensures that stigma remains intact, regularization does not ensure its removal, since problems with stigma remain even in decriminalized jurisdictions like New Zealand (Abel, 2011). Laws and policies must therefore be implemented with an eye to the role of stigma and the importance of addressing it head-on in order to ensure effective policy. For example, stigma means that there will be sizable resistance to the location of sex businesses, which will tempt local governments in particular to squeeze the industry into limited zones and/or restrict the number of operators. Stigma can also act to inform paternalistic policy approaches that deny sex workers' agency and voice so that their ability to move freely within the industry or launch legal actions are severely restricted. However, these practices, as we shall see, have a number of negative consequences that undermine policy goals. Policies should ensure that sex workers have maximum access to tools for self-empowerment, including complaint mechanisms, the ability to move between workplaces, and useful knowledge on the operation of the law and their rights. The formulation of effective and just policies will therefore require the close involvement and participation of both sex workers and management.

Bringing the Industry in from the Cold

Ultimately, of course, encouraging good management practices will require bringing the sex industry in from the cold and in line with the general practices of business and labour regulation. However, this step is not as straightforward as simply removing criminal laws. The sex industry, as Wagenaar et al. (2013) have pointed out, is not a "compliant" industry – it has, rather, long been engaged in a combative or furtive relationship with the state, one that is unlikely to change overnight. It will require hard work over time to build communication and trust – much of which will depend on good policymaking and consultation. There are indeed unique features to the sex industry – including this history of exclusion – that must be addressed for policies to function well. As Kavemann and Rabe (2007) have argued, one of the problems consistently found in sex-industry-related policymaking is policymakers' tendency to shy away from making things better for managers of sex businesses (who are viewed as inherently problematic), when in fact managers can only be required to uphold decent working conditions if they themselves are assured of being treated fairly under the law and are free to make a profit. For example, brothel managers and owners need to have planning certainty (e.g., the granting, except under very specific conditions – such as a record of violent crimes towards workers – of permits and licences) if they are going to establish businesses that also uphold safety and labour regulations.

In many cases, however, planning certainty has been very difficult to establish, largely because of pushback from municipal governments who have a tendency to use their regulatory power to limit or suppress sex businesses, even under regulated or decriminalized conditions. Indeed, as Wagenaar and Altink (2012) explain, debates around sex industry policies constitute "morality politics" par excellence: resistant to facts, highly emotional, and with little institutional knowledge or expertise to get in the way. Local governments are particularly vulnerable to the morality politics around sex work because disputes over sex work often centre on municipally controlled issues such as zoning and the use of public places. Further, local governments can pay a price if there is no higher-level government policy standardizing the treatment of sex businesses across jurisdictions. Left to their own devices, municipalities engage in a race to the bottom imposing the most restrictive policies in order to ensure that they are not the recipient of an "undesirable industry" pushed out of other locations. Thus, in the absence of specific policies enacted by higher-level governments, municipalities often face enormous pressure to restrict the sex industry through fees or regulatory mechanisms. This in turn results in frustrations and difficulties for owners/manager who try to apply for licences or zoning permits and a temptation to remain "out in the cold" (Crofts, 2010). This is particularly true for small owner-operators who do not have the money, political leverage, or resources to fight battles with city hall or meet restrictive municipal standards. The end result can be the establishment of oligopolistic control over the industry which, as we will see later, can act in many ways to limit and undermine sex workers' workplace rights.

In the Netherlands, New Zealand, and parts of Australia, where criminal restrictions on brothels were lifted in an attempt to improve working conditions, municipalities became very active in zoning out and restricting sex businesses. In the Netherlands, the government assumed that after lifting its ban on brothels, the choice of occupation enshrined in the constitution would prevent municipalities from trying to ban the industry outright. Nonetheless, 12 per cent of Dutch municipalities tried to impose a total ban (only to be later ruled out of order by the courts) and numerous others moved to freeze and/or reduce to the absolute minimum the number of establishments in their jurisdictions (Government of Norway, 2004). Analysts have concluded that the resulting restriction on businesses has stifled innovation in the industry, including the development of new initiatives, such as sex worker cooperatives, that would greatly improve sex workers' working conditions (Daalder, 2007). In the Australian state of New South Wales, where brothels are not licensed but do require council consent, Crofts (2010) documents tighter restrictions on parking, disability access, operating hours, and zoning that other businesses with similar "amenity impacts" are not asked to meet. Thus many owners who have found themselves refused have had to appeal to the court in order to establish their right to operate legally (Crofts, 2010; Donovan et al., 2012; Smith, 2003). In 1999 it was found that most brothels operating legally had managed to receive consent only by launching a court case (Donovan et al., 2012). Thus the system of regularization became much more expensive and difficult than it should have been, discouraging sex businesses from applying for council consent as the barriers were seen as too high and the application would only draw attention to their existence (Crofts, 2010). Already in Canada's semi-regulated sex industry sector – escort, body rub, erotic dance, and so on – some cities have moved to restrict these businesses to particular zones and licensing fees are frequently set at very high levels (Law, this collection; see also Gardner, 2002; Lowman, 2005). While some court decisions have challenged discriminatory licensing practices, the bias towards moral regulation in Canadian municipalities is clear from the adoption of a variety of mechanisms to limit the trade above and beyond the criminal law, including so-called john-shaming campaigns, traffic-diversion schemes, and the use of injunctions (Barnett, 2011). The underlying moralism of sex work regulation, which is fueled by the desire to punish "badly behaved" women, results in policies that move to sweep away the trade while failing to recognize the possibilities of policies that render the trade safer and less exploitative (Auger, 2014; Sanders, 2005). In the Canadian context this has led to many municipalities adopting policies, such as john schools and street sweeps, that worsen sex workers' positions (Shaver, Lewis, and Maticka-Tyndale, 2005). The moral focus of such regulation creates fewer options for sex workers and decreases incentives for managers to cooperate with regulatory regimes.

Importantly, such a restrictive approach is particularly difficult for single owner-operator or small home-based businesses. Restrictions may be intentional (zoning that limits sex businesses to industrial zones, for example), or unintentional (the failure to adopt policies that are sensitive to the particular situation of small sex businesses). In New South Wales, while home-based businesses make up some 40 per cent of operations, they are sometimes defined as "brothels" and treated the same way as large businesses. Home-based businesses could therefore be required to put a sign on the lawn advertising the nature of their development application – a sure way to draw neighbourhood attention and opprobrium. They might also be required to ensure that they are not located near other homes, a very difficult condition to meet in many urban areas. According to Crofts (2010), "these kinds of planning requirements make it virtually impossible for home occupations (sex services) to apply for, let alone receive, development consent" (155). Research has shown, however, that these small businesses have little or no amenity impact on neighbourhoods and are generally safer and more amenable for sex workers (Prior and Crofts, 2015; New South Wales, 2006). Moreover, the flourishing of smaller and/or home-based establishments is an important source of pressure on larger operators to adopt good workplace policies as it gives sex workers the ability to vote with their feet and/or set up their own businesses more to their liking if conditions in larger operations are not up to par.

There is not only the problem of resistance by municipalities but the lack of expertise and resources to develop and implement appropriate regulations. In New South Wales – where the state government barred municipalities from issuing blanket prohibitions on sex businesses, but did not develop guidelines on those policies – only the largest city, Sydney, was able to develop and implement a fairly progressive and effective policy. Thus many sex businesses in New South Wales continue to operate "without council consent," (i.e., illegally). This is in large part because many municipalities were very slow to develop planning regulations around brothels and waited instead for state-level guidelines. Similarly, owners were slow to apply for council consent until these issues had been clarified so that they could be certain of what conditions they would have to meet. By 2003, eight years after brothels were decriminalized, only 50 per cent of municipalities in New South Wales had worked out brothel planning regulations (and most of these tended to restrict operation to particular zones). In the Netherlands, similarly, municipalities left to struggle on their own developed a patchwork of approaches and enforcement procedures, which resulted in the migration of "illegal" or unregulated forms of the industry into jurisdictions perceived as less restrictive (Daalder, 2007). Wagenaar (2006) argues that while the Dutch government later stepped in with model contracts and licences, and facilitated cooperation between government branches, the initial problem was caused by the failure to bring municipalities into policy discussions from the beginning and therefore leaving them to cope with a complex policy issue on their own.

As Crofts (2010) points out, however, Sydney's experience suggests that it is indeed possible to develop sound planning principles that bring sex businesses into the ambit of law and regulation and facilitate improved health and safety, good working conditions, and reduced amenity impacts (see City of Sydney DCP, 2006). The guidelines formulated by the city of Sydney distinguish small from large sex businesses, requiring council consent only for large operations (with over four employees), and created conditions for "safe house brothels" (essentially a safe place for street-based workers to take clients) that work to reduce violence against street-based workers.[1] The Sydney council employs a sex industry liaison to help build open communication and trust between the industry and the municipality. The council's planning guidelines have worked so effectively over the past several years that the number of objections to brothels applying for council consent has dropped dramatically as citizens now recognize that brothels and smaller sex businesses can operate in their neighbourhoods without creating a problem, and that the city will indeed act to rectify any ensuing issues or shut down problematic businesses. Sex business owners and managers, now treated as citizens, also feel they can turn to police when the need arises: for example, one brothel owner reported extortion threats by a local biker gang to the police (Crofts, 2010).

New Zealand's success in convincing brothels to come in from the cold lay in part in a careful policy groundwork that recognized the importance of not adopting a punitive approach towards sex businesses and recognizing the needs of operators to be able to function as a business (while balancing this with community "amenity concerns"). Restrictions on signage have been limiting but not prohibitive according to Knight (2010). For example, some municipalities direct that the signs may only contain the name of the business, while others, such as Wellington, the capital, insist on approving all signs. Advertising is also limited so that sex businesses may not explicitly advertise on radio, television, or film, though websites are not addressed in the regulation. Print media advertising in classified sections is now possible (it was often refused before decriminalization) (Government of New Zealand, 2008). Brothels may advertise for staff and use the word *brothel*, in contrast to older, more obscure ads that may have made the type of work unclear (Abel, Fitzgerald et al., 2010). All of this has made it easier for brothels to operate.

Further, instead of using licensing to control businesses, New Zealand adopted a far less restrictive certification process, the purpose of which is to ensure that prospective operators do not have serious criminal records. The certification process is much less cumbersome and punitive than the licensing of businesses, thus encouraging operators to become regularized. It targets the actual problem – the possibility that operators might be violent offenders – rather than using licensing to restrict the number of businesses. The certification process was designed to avoid expense and difficulty (Mossman, 2010). All brothel operators (owners, managers, receptionists) must pay NZ$200 for a certificate in order to legally manage a brothel – although small owner-operated brothels (SOOBs) are exempted. If an operator has been convicted of a serious crime the certificate can be denied or revoked. Operators' identities are closely guarded, even from police. Importantly, certificates are linked to individual third parties (including receptionists, who are considered to be in a position of some authority), not to the specific businesses' site (i.e., it is an operators' licence). Thus the legislation is designed to address some of the stigma faced by operators and to build trust between the state and operators (Abel et al., 2010). The certification process is therefore seen as working fairly well, neither discouraging operators from coming in from the cold nor creating an illegal parallel industry (Mossman, 2010).

Certainly, such a certification process has advantages over a licensing regime that, as van der Meulen and Valverde (2013) have argued, gives enormous powers to municipalities. In Canada the licensing process works to limit and/or place unreasonable burdens on businesses because licences are viewed in law as a "privilege" and therefore the licence holder can be "subject to all sorts of rules that wouldn't be legal in other circumstances" (320). Licensing schemes for individual sex workers have already been widely critiqued in the literature (Chapkis, 1997; Lewis and Maticka-Tyndale, 2000), but licensing for businesses also poses problems even beyond their inconsistent and often moralistic fee structures. Licensing schemes tend to heavily involve police in the regulation of the industry, which creates the danger that the information provided for licensing will be used in criminal investigations and/or civil court proceedings (Lewis and Maticka-Tyndale, 2000; Laing, 2012). As we have seen in previous chapters on the incall/outcall and strip club sectors, the licences already in use in Canada for erotic dance clubs and massage parlours have not necessarily resulted in higher standards of cleanliness and safety and have often increased risks for sex workers (see also Auger, 2014; Bruckert and Law, 2013; Laing, 2012). Combined with the continued stigma around the sex industry, such powers in the hands of municipalities mitigate against the establishment of fair and reasonable standards for sex industry businesses that would facilitate their regularization.

The adoption of good practices in the sex industry must therefore involve careful education and encouragement rather than standard rule-setting and enforcement. Policymakers also have to realize that improving practices means increased costs for managers and owners. Moreover, they must recognize that if there is to be a "viable market sector" with competitive businesses and innovation, then measures should be taken to ensure that these increased costs are not overly onerous; these could include, for example, incentives for coming up to code and investments in buildings and safety features. Otherwise, increased demands and resistance to service from other government sectors results in a "disincentive for investment and innovation," which is precisely what is needed in order for sex workers' rights and safety to be best protected (Butt and Salazar, 2004, 4). Further, a consolidation of the industry reduces sex worker autonomy and gives greater control to a few, financially well off, managers (rather than "good" managers[2]) (Butt and Salazar, 2004). Policymaking should be focused on encouraging good practices rather than simply punishing those who do not come up to snuff (particularly when it comes to "minor" matters such as zoning infractions), which only discourages owners/managers from transitioning into legal practice. The encouragement of smaller (owner-operator) businesses is an important tool in facilitating the adoption of best practices. Careful attention must be paid to the impact of stigma on such operations in the application of by-laws and licensing requirements – for example, the standard requirements for zoning hearings and applications can generate negative public exposure and opposition that is exceptionally difficult for small owner-operated businesses to cope with (Crofts, 2010).

Governments clearly have a role to play in establishing a level playing field for sex businesses within and across jurisdictions. Given the Canadian division of powers between federal and provincial governments, regulation of the industry will fall to the provinces once sex work is no longer a criminal matter. While the federal government will no longer be able to legislate, it can use its powers to encourage best practices among the provinces via information sharing and the creation of bureaucratic expertise as well as using its funding powers to encourage common initiatives in the sex industry. Municipalities are dependent on provincial governments for mandates and funding; provinces could therefore be called upon to ensure that all municipalities within their jurisdiction are upholding common practices. Federal and provincial authorities in Canada will need to encourage municipalities to establish common practices in regards to sex businesses that both enable the development of a variety of set ups (including smaller operations) within a reasonable range of locales and create a reasonable level of planning certainty to encourage these businesses to engage in the regularization process. The broadest possible jurisdictional standards also enable the efficient and effective use of oversight procedures so that all stakeholders, including managers, owners, workers, government officials, police, and inspectors, have a shared knowledge and understanding of best practices and procedures, no matter what jurisdiction they are working in. Further, as Daalder (2007) points out, many operations are national or even international in scope; the reliance on local municipalities for oversight and regulation is therefore limited. In addition, higher levels of government can make an important contribution by assisting in the development of best practices and guidelines for already overburdened municipal governments often unprepared to deal with such a complex policy issue. These best practices must of course be developed in consultation with sex workers themselves. PIVOT Legal Society (2006) has argued that – along with educating bureaucrats and police, making licensing fees fair, providing avenues of legal redress, and ensuring the protection of privacy – governments should fund a sex-worker task force to provide input on appropriate municipal regulations. As Wagenaar and Altink (2012) have argued, the creation of institutionalized expertise on sex-trade policy issues within government, as well as building up relations of trust with the sex industry, is key to the establishment of workable policy.

Regulating Employer-Employee Relations

The point, of course, of bringing sex businesses in from the cold is to establish better working conditions for sex workers in terms of health and safety, as well as protecting their labour rights. Even under criminalized conditions there is movement to address sex workers' labour rights, including by incorporating sex workers under international labour standards via the International Labour Organization, and through groundbreaking court cases such as the Kylie case in South Africa, which has ruled sex workers are employees even in a criminalized industry (Overs and Loff, 2013; Selala, 2011). The hope is that a regularized industry would create the opportunity to establish standard employment conditions.[3] However, standard employer-employee relationships may be difficult to institute in the sex industry. Because of the importance of sexual consent there are limits on what managers can and should control (e.g., engaging in particular sex acts or seeing particular clients), which may "make traditional business structures seem inapplicable" (Butt and Salazar, 2004, 4). The sex industry, in Canada as elsewhere, has become accustomed to operating via a freelancer model – in part because this is currently seen to protect sex workers, to some degree, from criminal charges (Bruckert and Law, 2013; Law, this collection; PIVOT Legal Society, 2006). And, as we have seen in this study, there is quite a gradation of control over the labour process exercised by agencies and associates, making any clear distinction between employee and freelancer difficult to ascertain. As Agustin (2008) has rightly pointed out, no matter what its legal status, the industry is indeed a flexible labour market par excellence and this flexibility is a key reason that many people work in the industry – stricter employee status can easily create a migration back into the unregulated sector. Importantly, however, as Tuulia Law detailed in Chapter 5, the blurring of lines between "employee" and "contractor" has been a central feature of current employment practices, particularly in the feminized service sector (e.g., sales associates, care providers) (see Fudge, Tucker, and Vosko, 2003; Bruckert and Law, this collection). Managers' ability to argue that sex workers are freelancers and not employees, despite the fact that managers control shifts, dress, and codes of behaviour, has undermined sex workers' labour rights while creating greater profits. The flexibility of sex work, while it is one of the sector's attractions, also opens up the possibility of exploitation of labour when owners/managers exert control over the labour process without treating employees as actual employees – resulting in "flexibilization" and precariousness rather than flexibility, as is the case in so many other industries in the neo-liberal era.

It has traditionally been held that the introduction of standard employment contracts will resolve problems of worker exploitation in the sex industry. However, as policymakers in Germany discovered, the benefits of employment contracts cannot be assumed. Germany introduced "one-sided" contracts that allowed sex workers to sue clients for failure to pay but did not allow clients to sue sex workers for unsatisfactory services. Similarly, employers are obligated to pay salaries and provide benefits but cannot demand that sex workers accept a particular client or provide a particular service (Kavemann and Rabe, 2007). However, there was some resistance even from sex workers to the idea of contracts, first because of the breach of anonymity involved, and second because of the move to regular pay rather than the per-client pay to which sex workers were accustomed (Bretzlaff, 2008; Klee, 2005). Further, it was assumed by policymakers that sex workers would prefer employment contracts because they entail benefits, including health insurance provisions. However, it turned out that many workers already had private insurance through other mechanisms, and that they did not want pension deductions because they assumed they would be working in the industry only a short time (Kavemann and Rabe, 2007). For managers, the contracts were problematic because of their one-sided nature and because there was little instruction/communication on the use of contracts in an industry where there is limited experience with such legally binding agreements and where suspicion of government regulation is high (Klee, 2005).

In New Zealand employment contracts have also been difficult to develop and enforce, and most brothel workers continue to be classified as freelance workers rather than employees. There has also been some resistance to written contracts altogether, as workers have expressed concern that written (rather than verbal) contracts might involve demands for services they are unwilling to provide – although this would not in fact be permissible under current New Zealand law, the fear remains. Further, even in a decriminalized industry, employees have been unwilling so far to challenge poor contracts or breaches of contract at the Employment Court because of fear of exposure: contracts, of course, are no guarantee against stigma. The practice of bonding and/or fining workers has continued in a few places, even in New Zealand's decriminalized environment (Government of New Zealand, 2008; Mossman, 2010). The Prostitution Law Reform Committee

(PLRC) charged with reviewing the effects of the legal revisions in New Zealand has suggested that, rather than enforcing contracts or outright banning the use of bonds, the government should provide managers with education in best practices so as to avoid pushing the industry underground once again (Government of New Zealand, 2008). Mossman (2010) points out that managers may, for example, need encouragement to try forms of workplace discipline more commonly practised elsewhere, such as a system of warnings before dismissal rather than fines. Indeed, the PLRC has argued that while older operations have continued in their set practices, sex establishments that have opened up since the industry was decriminalized have been more likely to adopt good employment practices (Government of New Zealand, 2008).

Clearly, the development and maintenance of employment contracts as part of the regularization process will require give and take on the part of both employers and employees, as it does in any other industry. However, the regulation of the employer-employee relationship in the sex industry is not unrelated to the ways in which sex industry management is dealt with more generally, as the purposeful or inadvertent creation of an oligopoly of owners in the industry bodes poorly for the creation of good working conditions. Owners used to resisting and/or avoiding government intervention can also effectively oppose new labour conditions. In the Netherlands, for example, the ban on brothels was lifted, but a small and powerful group of owners was created through restrictive licensing: the government found itself unable to force owners to accept employment contracts, even though many workers fit the definition of employee rather than freelance worker. The tax department, for one, which eventually accepted the employers' argument that the workers were self-employed, classified them under a special category that was supposed to ensure the sex workers are able to, for example, set their own hours, refuse clients or particular sexual acts, and choose their own clothing. However, because these conditions did not bring the regulation under the ambit of labour law, there were no complaints procedures or sanctions for breeching these conditions (Wagenaar et al., 2013). Unsurprisingly, then, conditions even in the licensed sector remained unimproved, and many of these stipulations are frequently breeched (Wagenaar et al., 2013). Avoiding overly restrictive licensing conditions is therefore key to establishing good employment conditions.

In the same vein, one must also be cautious of the overly zealous application of health and safety or employment regulations, which could well be viewed as the unfair targeting of an "unwanted" industry. In New South Wales some of those sex businesses that did receive council consent complained that they were over-regulated in comparison to other businesses; though they often faced intrusive inspections and sometimes raids (where planning bodies are accompanied by immigration or police officials, giving municipal officers much greater access than justified under planning provisions), illegal businesses were not targeted for closure or disciplinary action. This created tension in the industry, both among operators and between operators and the municipality. Finally, some legal operations found that the well-meaning insertion of health and safety guidelines in planning requirements had resulted in over-regulation via "micro-level compliance actions" (e.g., fines and overly frequent inspections) that undermined the very effectiveness of health and safety procedures that had been achieved previously through voluntary compliance (New South Wales, 2006, 45–6). Once again, for a stigmatized and previously targeted industry, this only creates further tension and distrust between government and operators and discourages cooperation. Policymakers need to be vigilant about such "hyper" or unfair application of rules and regulations. This is already taking place in Canada to the extent that the by-law burden faced by service businesses is typically quite onerous (van der Meulen and Valverde, 2013). Particular attention needs to be paid to the development and application of such rules for smaller owner-operator businesses. As van der Meulen and Valverde (2013) have pointed out, current by-laws targeting escort agencies in Canada can already make life particularly difficult for smaller operations. For example, Edmonton by-laws requiring escort agency office doors to remain unlocked during business hours makes running a single owner-operator business extremely difficult. Such practices undermine the potential of small operations to establish good working conditions and their ability to pressure other businesses to do the same.

There are also ways to address precarious labour conditions outside of a full employment contract that can avoid the heavy-handedness of contract law. Precariousness is a condition shared by workers in a number of different sectors in the Canadian economy. In looking at a variety of forms of precarious labour in Ontario, Vosko, Tucker, and Mark (2011) have recommended a number of ways to expand and strengthen guidelines laid out in the *Occupational Health and Safety Act* and the *Employment Standards Act* to more effectively protect those working in precarious work, including adopting "proactive enforcement" of "high-violation" industries by strengthening the inspections and investigations of workplaces, protecting complainants from retaliation, and giving voice to workers by involving worker advocates and community organizations in the oversight process. The New Zealand PLRC has pointed to the need for "properly funded NGOs to act as brokers for sex workers as they access mainstream services" (PLRC, para. 10.7) The PLRC also suggested employment-law training (and the funding for this) be provided to these NGOs so that they can more effectively assist sex workers in building relationships with government agencies and challenging poor working conditions (PLRC para. 10.7; see also PIVOT Legal Society, 2006 for Canadian recommendations). Drawing on the work of the Australian sex worker organization Scarlet Alliance, the New Zealand government worked together with the New Zealand Prostitutes' Collective to draft its very effective occupational health and safety guidelines for the industry (van der Meulen, 2011).

As van der Meulen (2011) has argued, Canada's current occupational health and employment policies need modification if they are to reflect the particular concerns of sex workers. However, Gillies (2013) has noted that there are a number of health and safety guidelines currently in use at Canadian workplaces that would be useful for sex work establishments, including the formalization of the right to refuse dangerous work without reprisal, safety procedures (particularly for those working alone), as well as protocols reducing workplace violence that require businesses to document incidents and make workers aware of risks and how to handle them. Further, human rights codes forbidding discriminatory hiring practices need to be upheld within the sex industry (Gillies, 2013). The formation of unions or sector-wide associations, while not without its struggles, would also go a long way towards establishing better working conditions and upholding standards (Clamen, Gillies, and Salah, 2013; Gillies, 2013; PIVOT Legal Society, 2006; van der Meulen, 2011). Certainly, alternate forms of worker organization have been explored and can be encouraged through progressive policy and law (Vosko, 2000). Looking at the success of the Scarlet Alliance in Australia, Gall has argued that sex workers can build on already existing forms of "independent collectivism" to negotiate labour conditions (Gall, 2014).

Whether workers are organized or not, there should be feedback and grievance mechanisms that – again, taking careful account of the role of stigma in the industry – enable workers to voice complaints and launch legal actions when needed. While relying on individual complaints to trigger oversight or regulation is a limited approach, it is important to provide some form of feedback to regulatory bodies, both to inform policy and to alert such bodies to potentially exploitative practices. One of the great weaknesses of Queensland, Australia's Prostitution Licensing Authority is the lack of any sort of input from sex workers concerning workplace complaints (Sullivan, 2010). The system remains focused on rooting criminal elements out of the sex industry rather than addressing sex workers' workplace concerns. Governments also need to support sex workers in their ability to launch legal challenges where necessary. Once again, this could mean supporting sex worker NGOs as they assist in the process. It could also involve a return to legal-assistance programs that enable marginalized individuals to launch important court challenges. Finally, governments need to find ways to enhance the working conditions of those in more independent sectors by, for example, making pensions and benefits available to individuals who prefer to work outside the brothel/agency structure. Governments could also support the formation of cooperatives with formalized structures that enable access to pensions and workers' compensation schemes while simultaneously acting as a professional association or lobby group (PIVOT Legal Society, 2006). The more viable and safe options there are for sex workers, the more pressure there will be on management to uphold high employment standards.

We can also look beyond the direct regulation of businesses to broader issues affecting sex workers' negotiating power, especially their ability to address their socio-economic status. Recognizing the role stigma plays in denying sex workers' rights – not only in employment but in day-to-day life – should lead policymakers to examine the role of banking institutions, insurance companies, landlords, and so on, who sometimes deny services because of stigma, thereby limiting sex workers' options. Access to housing, loans, financial instruments, and insurance are key to improving sex workers' economic and social well-being and to enabling effective negotiation with employers – but again, this may be denied to them, even if their occupation is no longer criminalized, because of long-standing attitudes and biases (Overs and Loff, 2013). Here governments can move to legally protect sex workers from discrimination. Queensland, for example, banned the denial of services or housing to sex workers on the basis of occupational discrimination (Jeffrey and Sullivan, 2009). These sorts of wide-reaching policies can have a marked effect on sex workers' status as employees and citizens and give them a much stronger basis from which to negotiate good working conditions.

Working closely with the sex work community is the best way to establish guidelines and best practices in the industry. A number of sex worker organizations have come up with guidelines that should form the basis of industry-specific employment practices. The British Columbia Coalition of Experiential Communities (BCCEC), for example, has published guidelines for owners in the sex industry in their *Trade Secrets* guide. The organization has also suggested a system of rewards rather than punishments for owners/managers that meet their guidelines. In its 2007 report *Developing Capacity for Change*, the BCCEC also created models for cooperative businesses in the sex industry (Arthur, Davis, and Shannon, 2013; see also PIVOT Legal Society, 2006). Sex worker organizations have been key in establishing effective health and safety guidelines in both New Zealand and New South Wales. These guidelines highlight sex workers' health and safety concerns – such as client violence and safety and security measures – that, as we saw in Chapter 4, are sometimes overlooked by managers (Government of New Zealand, 2004). Policy processes that maximize sex worker involvement will help to create procedures that most accurately reflect the particularities of the sex industry and protect and promote sex workers' rights.

Unfortunately, since the passing of new laws criminalizing the purchase of sexual services and third party involvement in late 2014, the policy climate in Canada has undermined many of the possible roads forward. Nonetheless, there are some signs that municipalities and sex workers are trying to negotiate workable conditions. The city of Vancouver, for example, has seen the slow build-up of what Fuji-Johnson (2015) has termed an "agonistic" policy community, wherein government and activists have, in spite of deep divisions, been able to make some progress on working together. To take one recent example, in 2015 the city issued its *Sex Work Response Guidelines*, developed in collaboration with sex worker groups, to promote respect and non-discrimination towards sex workers and to "build positive relationships with individuals and businesses engaged in the sex industry." These guidelines include some positive signs of the city's recognition of some of the issues raised here, including the importance of addressing stigma (by not alerting media about raids on sex establishments and respecting the confidentiality of "experiential persons"); keeping the health and safety of sex workers top of mind in the regulation of the industry (the presence of safer sex materials is explicitly excluded as a by-law infringement); consulting the sex work community in creating policy; and maintaining proportionality and transparency when enforcement actions are taken against licensed businesses (City of Vancouver, 2015). How these guidelines will play out in practice over the coming years remains to be seen. But they nonetheless provide an example of some of the positive steps that can be taken at the municipal level, and the possibilities for building a base for collaboration, even in the face of the continuing criminalization of the sex trade.

Concluding Reflections

Governments have a very important role to play in establishing good management practices and working conditions in the Canadian sex industry. Federal laws in Canada that directly criminalize managers and clients have created enormous barriers to creating fair and safe sex work policies, but there are lessons to be drawn for the future. Policy-making in this area is not easy, and it will require the building up of expertise at the provincial and federal levels in order to ensure that policies are not undermined by unintended effects. First and foremost, however, governments need to shift attitudinal biases away from the suppression of the industry by treating both managers and workers as part of the making and implementation of policy. Second, federal and provincial governments will have to ensure that morality politics and lack of capacity do not undermine attempts to regularize the sex industry. Thus, governments must make certain that policies do not, whether intentionally or unintentionally, have a negative impact on industry innovations like the development of cooperatives or small owner-operator/home-based businesses. In doing so, they will have to counteract the tendency among municipalities to squeeze the industry either through zoning restrictions or hefty regulations. Governments should instead encourage a wide range of choices of workplace in order to maximize sex workers' rights and safety. In Canada, this would require leadership from federal and provincial governments in setting best practices and/or standardized policies to avoid the "race to the bottom" effect (between provinces as well as municipalities) occasioned by local morality politics. It would also require an investment of resources and expertise so that municipalities are not left to struggle on their own in a complex policy area. Finally, creativity and close cooperation with workers and management will also be required in establishing good working conditions within the sex industry, which perhaps includes looking beyond standard employment contracts as the best or only method of improving labour conditions. In all policy decisions governments will need to tackle stigma as a major obstacle to developing sound practices, something that can only begin by treating management and sex workers as part of the solution rather than the problem.

Notes

1 Safe house brothels mean that sex workers can avoid servicing clients in dangerous locations (cars, out-of-the-way places) and have access to a variety of security systems (alarms, controlled entrances, intercoms) to both prevent and respond to client violence.
2 "Good" management in this context includes practices that effectively protect sex workers' safety, security, and emotional and physical health, as well as their financial well-being. See Bruckert and Law (2013) for sex workers' own identification of good practices.
3 PIVOT Legal Society (2006) has laid out in some detail how current BC Employment Standards and Occupational Health and Safety provisions could be adopted for use in the sex industry as long as sex workers' privacy concerns and right to sexual consent are protected.

Works Cited

Abel, G. 2011. "Different, stage, different performance: The protective strategy of role play on emotional health in sex work." *Social Science & Medicine*, 72 (7): 1177–84. https://doi.org/10.1016/j.socscimed.2011.01.021

Abel, G., and L. Fitzgerald. 2010. "Risk and risk management in sex work post-Prostitution Reform Act: A public health perspective." In *Taking the crime out of sex work: New Zealand sex workers' fight for decriminalisation*, edited by G. Abel, L. Fitzgerald, C. Healy, and A. Taylor, 217–38. Bristol, UK: Polity Press. https://doi.org/10.1332/policypress/9781847423344.003.0013.

Abel, G., L. Fitzgerald, C. Healy, and A. Taylor, eds. 2010. *Taking the crime out of sex work: New Zealand sex workers' fight for decriminalisation*. Bristol, UK: Policy Press.

Abel, G., C. Healy, C. Bennachie, and A. Reed. 2010. "The Prostitution Reform Act." In *Taking the crime out of sex work: New Zealand sex workers' fight for decriminalisation*, edited by G. Abel, L. Fitzgerald, C. Healy, and A. Taylor, 75–84. Portland, OR: Policy Press.

Agustin, L. 2008. "Sex and the limits of enlightenment: The irrationality of legal regimes to control prostitution." *Sexuality Research & Social Policy*, 5 (4): 73–86. https://doi.org/10.1525/srsp.2008.5.4.73

Althorp, J. 2013. "Beyond the stage: A gaze into the working lives of exotic stage dancers in Western Canada." MA thesis, Simon Fraser University.

Anderson, E. 1999. *Code of the street: Decency, violence, and the moral life of the inner city*. New York: W. W. Norton.

Appleby, T. 2000. "Three set for trial in Detroit deaths of Ontario teens." *Globe and Mail* (Toronto), 15 May.

AP [Associated Press]. 2008. "Mansion Madam's million-dollar home for sale." *Guardian* (Charlottetown), 28 February.

Arthur, J., S. Davis, and E. Shannon. 2013. "Overcoming challenges: Vancouver's sex worker movement." In *Selling sex: Experience, advocacy, and research on sex work in Canada*, edited by E. van der Meulen, E. M. Durisin, and V. Love, 130–46. Vancouver: UBC Press.

Attorney General of Canada. 2011. Factum of the Appellant, the Attorney General of Canada (*Canada (Attorney General) v. Bedford*, 2012 ONCA 186).

Auger, C. 2014. "Criminalized and licensed: Local politics, the regulation of sex work, and the construction of 'ugly bodies.' " In *Negotiating sex work*, edited by C. R. Showden and S. Majic, 99–120. Minneapolis: University of Minnesota Press.

Barnett, L. (2011) 2014. "Prostitution in Canada: International obligations, federal law and provincial and municipal jurisdiction." Background Paper No 2011–119-E. http://www.parl.gc.ca/Content/LOP/Research Publications/2011-119-e.htm#txt111.

Baron, D. P. 2006. "Persistent media bias." *Journal of Public Economics*, 90(1–2): 1–36. https://doi.org/10.1016/j.jpubeco.2004.10.006

Barry, K. 1995. "Pimping: The world's oldest profession." *On the Issues Magazine*, 4 (3): 42–9.

Barton, B. 2006. *Stripped: Inside the lives of exotic dancers.* New York: NYU Press.

Béland, G. 2013. "Boxeur ou bon gars de l'année?" *La Presse* (Montreal), 10 December.

Bell, C., and F. Ward. 2013. "Ratchet me this: How do we ride for pleasure in a pimp culture?" *Real Colored Girls* (blog). https://realcoloredgirls.wordpress .com/2013/12/22/ratchet-me-this-how-do-we-ride-for-pleasure-in-a-pimp -culture-2/

Benoit, C., C. Atchison, L. Casey, B. Jansson, B. McCarthy, R. Phillips, and F. Shaver. 2014. "Gender, violence and health: Contexts of vulnerabilities, resiliencies and care among people in the sex industry." Working paper prepared as background to Building on the evidence: An international symposium on the sex industry in Canada, Ottawa, ON.

Benson, J. 2012. "Myths about pimps: Conflicting images of hypermasculine pimps in US American hip-hop and bisexual pimps in the novels of Donald Goines and Iceberg Slim." *Journal of Bisexuality*, 12 (3): 429–41. https://doi .org/10.1080/15299716.2012.702627

Berg, B. 2009. *Qualitative methods for the social sciences*, 6th ed. Boston: Allynand Bacon.

Bernstein, E. 2007a. "The sexual politics of the 'new abolitionism.' " *Differences: A Journal of Feminist Cultural Studies*, 18 (3): 128–51. https://doi .org/10.1215/10407391-2007-013

Bernstein, E. 2007b. "Sex work for the middle classes." *Sexualities*, 10 (4): 473–88. https://doi.org/10.1177/1363460707080984

Bolton, S. C., and M. Houlihan. 2010. "Bermuda revisited? Management power and powerlessness in the worker-manager-customer triangle. *Work and Occupations*, 37 (3): 378–403. https://doi.org/10.1177/0730888410375678

Bouclin, S. 2004. "Exploited employees or exploited entrepreneurial agents? A look at erotic dancers. *Canadian Woman Studies*, 23 (3/4): 132–7.

Bouclin, S. 2006. "Dancers empowering (some) dancers: The intersections of race, class and gender in organizing erotic labourers." *Race, Gender, & Class*, 13 (3/4): 98–130.

Bouclin, S. 2009. "Bad girls like good contracts: Ontario erotic dancers' collective resistance." In *Victim no more: Women's resistance to law, culture and power*, edited by E. Faulkner and G. MacDonald, 46–60. Winnipeg: Fernwood Publishing.

Bowen, R., V. Bungay, C. Zangger. 2015. *Making SPACES: Advancing recommendations for the off-street sex industry in Vancouver*. Vancouver: Making SPACES project.

Boyd, T. 1997. *Am I black enough for you? Popular culture from the hood and beyond*. Bloomington: Indiana University Press.

Bradley-Engen, M. S., and C. M. Hobbs. 2010. "To love, honor, and strip: An investigation of exotic dancer romantic relationships." In *Sex work matters: Exploring money, power, and intimacy in the sex industry*, edited by Melissa Hope, Ditmore Antonia, and Levy Alys, 67–84. New York: Zed Books.

Brents, B., and K. Hausbeck. 2005. "Violence and legalized brothel prostitution in Nevada: Examining safety, risk and prostitution policy." *Journal of Interpersonal Violence*, 20 (3): 270–95. https://doi.org/10.1177/0886260504270333

Bretzlaff, A. 2008. "An examination of changing patterns of prostitution in Germany since unification." MA thesis, Carleton University.

Brock, D. 2009. *Making work, making trouble: The social regulation of sexual labour*. Toronto: University of Toronto Press.

Brooks, S. 2010. "Hypersexualization and the dark body: Race and inequality among Black and Latina women in the exotic dance industry." *Sexuality Research & Social Policy*, 7 (2): 70–80. https://doi.org/10.1007/s13178-010-0010-5

Brooks, S. 1997. "Dancing toward freedom." In *Whores and other feminists*, edited by J. Nagel, 252–55. New York: Routledge.

Bruckert, C. 2002. *Taking it off, putting it on: Women in the strip trade*. Toronto: Women's Press.

Bruckert, C. 2014. "Academic, activist, whore: Negotiating the insider-outsider abyss." In *Demarginalizing voices: Commitment, emotion and action in qualitative research*, edited by J. Kilty, S. Fabian, and M. Felices-Luna, 306–25. Vancouver: UBC Press.

Bruckert, C., and F. Chabot. 2010. *Challenges: Ottawa-area sex workers speak out.* Ottawa: POWER.

Bruckert, C., and M. Dufresne. 2002. "Reconfiguring the margins: Tracing the regulatory context of Ottawa strip clubs 1974–2000." *Canadian Journal of Law and Society*, 17 (1): 69–87. https://doi.org/10.1017/S0829320100007006

Bruckert, C., and S. Frigon. 2003. " 'Making a spectacle of herself': On women's bodies in the skin trades." *Atlantis: Critical Studies in Gender, Culture and Social Justice*, 28 (1): 48–62.

Bruckert, C., and S. Hannem. 2013. "Rethinking the prostitution debates: Transcending structural stigma in systemic responses to sex work." *Journal of Law and Society*, 28 (1): 43–63. https://doi.org/10.1017/cls.2012.2

Bruckert, C., and T. Law. 2013. *Beyond pimps, procurers and parasites: Mapping third parties in the incall/outcall sex industry.* Ottawa: Rethinking Management in the Adult and Sex Industry Project.

Bruckert, C., and C. Parent. 2007. "La danse érotique comme métier à l'ère de la vente de soi." *Cahiers de recherche sociologique*, 43: 95–107.

Bruckert, C., and C. Parent. 2014. Criminalized women workers: The in-call sex industry: Reflections on classed, gendered and racialized labour in the margins. In *Criminalizing women: Gender and (in)justice in neo-liberal times*, 2nd ed., edited by G. Balfour and E. Comack, 95–112. Winnipeg: Fernwood Press.

Bruckert, C., C. Parent, and P. Robitaille. 2003. *Erotic service/erotic dance establishments: Two types of marginalized labour.* Ottawa: University of Ottawa, Department of Criminology.

Burawoy, M. 1979. *Manufacturing consent: Changes in the labor process under monopoly capitalism.* Chicago: University of Chicago Press.

Büschi, E. 2010. "Sex work and violence: Focusing on managers in the indoor sex industry." *Sexualities*, 17 (5/6): 724–41.

Butt, L., and J. Salazar. 2004. "Lifting the ban: The oldest profession becomes the newest market sector." *Humanity in Action*. http://www.humanityinaction.org/knowledgebase/304-lifting-the-ban-the-oldest-profession-becomes-the-newest-market-sector

Chaleil, M. 1981. *Le corps prostitué.* Vol. 1, *Le sexe dévorant.* Paris: Les Éditions Galilée.

Cameron, S. 2002. "Criminals or victims, Hells Angels are staking their turf in Ontario." *Globe and Mail* (Toronto), 4 May.

Centre for Justice Statistics. 2016. *Family violence in Canada: A statistical profile, 2014.* Ottawa, ON: Centre for Justice Statistics.

Chapkis, W. 2000. "Power and control in the commercial sex trade." In *Sex for sale: Prostitution, pornography, and the sex industry*, edited by R. Weitzer, 181–201. New York: Routledge.

Chapkis, W. 1997. *Live sex acts: Women performing erotic labor*. New York: Routledge.

Childs, M., S. Ciarrocchi, C. Gleeson, J. Lowman, K. Pacey, F. Paradis, and L. Weich. 2006. *Beyond decriminalization: Sex work, human rights and a new framework for law reform*. Vancouver: Pivot Legal Society.

Chin, J. 2016. "Black man interviews white woman at Laval Tim Hortons, so someone calls 911." *Huffington Post* 29 February. http://www.huffingtonpost.ca/2016/02/27/mactar-mbaye-laval-tim-hortons_n_9336386.html

Choisy, M. 1961. *Psychoanalysis of the prostitute*. New York: Philosophical Library.

Chu, S., and R. Glass. 2013. "Sex work law reform in Canada: Considering problems with the Nordic model. *Alberta Law Review*, 51 (1): 101–24.

City of Sydney. DCP. 2006. "Adult entertainment and sex industry premises development control plan."

City of Vancouver. 2015. "City of Vancouver Sex Work Response Guidelines." http://vancouver.ca/files/cov/sex-work-response-guidelines.pdf

Clamen, J., C. Bruckert, and N. Mensah. 2013 *Managing sex work: Information for third parties and sex workers in the incall and outcall sectors of the sex industry*. Ottawa: Management Project.

Clamen, J, K. Gillies, and T. Salah. 2013. "Working for change: Sex workers in the union struggle." In *Selling sex: Experience, advocacy and research on sex work in Canada*, edited by E. van der Meulen, E. M. Durisin, and V. Love, 113–29. Vancouver: UBC Press.

Colosi, R. 2010a. *Dirty dancing? An ethnography of lap dancing*. New York: Willan.

Colosi, R. 2010b. " 'Just get pissed and enjoy yourself': Understanding lap dancing as 'anti-work.' " In *New sociologies of sex work*, edited by K. Hardy, S. Kingston, and T. Sanders, 181–96. Burlington, VT: Ashgate.

Comte, J. 2014. "Decriminalization of sex work: Feminist discourse in light of research." *Sexuality & Culture*, 18 (1): 196–217. https://doi.org/10.1007/s12119-013-9174-5

Couto, A. 2006. "Clothing exotic dancers with collective bargaining rights." *Ottawa Law Review*, 38 (1): 37–66.

CP [Canadian Press]. 2000. "Pimps convicted: Boxer and buddies held women in reign of terror." *Montreal Gazette*, 12 May.

CP [Canadian Press]. 2002. "Charges quashed against Toronto pimp because of 7-year court delay." *Globe and Mail* (Toronto), 24 April.

CP [Canadian Press]. 2004a. "Immigration d'effeuilleuses." *Le Soleil* (Québec), 8 December.

CP [Canadian Press]. 2004b. "Girl, 12, was forced into sex trade, police say." *Globe and Mail* (Toronto), 28 February.

Crofts, P. 2010. "Brothels: Outlaws or citizens?" *International Journal of Law in Context*, 6 (2): 151–66. https://doi.org/10.1017/S1744552310000054

Currie, N., and K. Gillies. 2006. "Bound by law: How Canada's protectionist public policies in the areas of both rape and prostitution limit women's choices, agency and activities." Unpublished report funded by Status of Women Canada.

Daalder, A. L. 2007. "Prostitution in the Netherlands since lifting of the brothel ban." Onderzoek en belied 249a. The Hague: Boom Juridische uitgevers, Wetenschappelijk Onderzoeken Documentatiecentrum.

Daft, R., and A. Armstrong. 2009. *Organization theory and design*, 1st. Canadian edition. Toronto: Nelson Education.

Dale, D. 2007. "Terry Koumoudouros, 67: Strip club owner." *Toronto Star*, 1 June.

Dalla, R. L. 2002. "Night moves: A qualitative investigation of street-level sex work." *Psychology of Women Quarterly*, 26 (1): 63–73. https://doi.org/10.1111/1471-6402.00044

Davidson, T. 2016. "Ajax man accused of pimping teen girl." *Toronto Sun*, 8 April. http://www.torontosun.com/2016/04/08/ajax-man-accused-of-pimping-teen-girl

Davidov, G. 2005. "Who is a worker?" *Industrial Law Journal*, 34 (1): 57–71. https://doi.org/10.1093/ilj/34.1.57

Davis, Angela. 1983. *Women, Race, and Class*. New York: Vintage.

Day, S. 2008. *Prostitution: Violating the human rights of poor women*. Ottawa: Action ontarienne contre la violence faite aux femmes.

DeMichele, M. T., and R. Tewksbury. 2004. "Sociological explorations in site-specific social control: The role of the strip club bouncer." *Deviant Behavior*, 25 (6): 537–58. https://doi.org/10.1080/01639620490484068

Denzin, N. K. 1978. *The research act: A theoretical introduction to sociological methods*. New York: McGraw-Hill.

Donovan, B., C. Harcourt, S. Egger, L. Watchirs Smith, K. Schneider, J. M. Kaldor, and S. Tabrizi. 2012. *The sex industry in New South Wales: A report to the NSW Ministry of Health*. Sydney, AU: Kirby Institute, University of New South Wales.

Dorais, M., and P. Corriveau. 2009. *Gangs and girls: Understanding juvenile prostitution*. Montreal: McGill-Queens University Press.

Doyle, C. 2011. *Dictionary of marketing*. Oxford: Oxford University Press.

Egan, R. D. 2006. "Resistance under the black light: Exploring the use of music in two exotic dance clubs." *Journal of Contemporary Ethnography*, 35 (2): 201–19. https://doi.org/10.1177/0891241605283570

Egan, R. D. 2004. "Eyeing the scene: The uses and (re)uses of surveillance cameras in an exotic dance club." *Critical Sociology*, 30 (2): 299–319. https://doi.org/10.1163/156916304323072125

Ekberg, G. 2014. "Presentation to the Standing Committee on Justice and Human Rights." Evidence of Proceedings, 41st Parl., 2nd sess., meetings no. 38.

Ericson, R., P. M. Baranek, and J. L. Chan. 1987. *Visualizing deviance: A study of news organization*. Toronto: University of Toronto Press.

Farley, M. 2003. "Prostitution and the invisibility of harm." *Women & Therapy*, 26 (3–4): 247–80. https://doi.org/10.1300/J015v26n03_06

Farley, M. 2004. " 'Bad for the body, bad for the heart': Prostitution harms women even if legalized or decriminalized." *Violence against Women*, 10 (10): 1087–1125. https://doi.org/10.1177/1077801204268607

Farley, M., A. Cotton, J. Lynne, S. Zumbeck, F. Spiwak, M. E. Reyes, and U. Sezgin. 2004. "Prostitution and trafficking in nine countries: Update on violence and posttraumatic stress disorder." *Journal of Trauma Practice*, 2 (3–4): 33–74. https://doi.org/10.1300/J189v02n03_03

Ferris, S. 2015. *Street sex work and Canadian cities: Resisting the dangerous order*. Edmonton: University of Alberta Press.

Fischer, C. B. 1996. "Employee rights in sex work: The struggle for dancers' rights as employees." *Law and Inequality: A Journal of Theory and Practice*, 14 (2): 521–54.

Fogel, C. A., and A. Quinlan. 2011. "Dancing naked: Precarious labour in the contemporary female strip trade." *Canadian Social Science*, 7 (5): 1–6.

Foucart, J. 2011. "Transaction sociale et gestion de l'intolérable. Une approche théorique de la déviance et du proxénétisme." *Pensée plurielle*, 27 (27): 29–41. https://doi.org/10.3917/pp.027.0029

Foucault, M. 1978. *The History of Sexuality*, vol. 1. New York: Pantheon Books.

Freeze, C. 2010. "Human trafficking rampant in Canada, RCMP reports." *Globe and Mail* (Toronto), 13 September.

Fudge, J., E. Tucker, and L. Vosko. 2003. "Employee or independent contractor? Charting the legal significance of the distinction in Canada." *Canadian Labour & Employment Law Journal*, 10 (2): 193–230.

Fudge, J., and L. Vosko. 2001. "By whose standards? Reregulating the Canadian labour market." *Economic and Industrial Democracy*, 22 (3): 327–356. https://doi.org/10.1177/0143831X01223002

Gadd, J. 2000. "Court told of teen's flight to escape sexual torment." *Globe and Mail* (Toronto), 3 May.

Gadd, J. 2001. "Sold as sex slave, woman tells court." *Globe and Mail* (Toronto), 26 April.

Gall, G. 2014. "Collective interest organization among sex workers." In *Negotiating sex work*, edited by C. Showden and S. Majic, 221–42. Minneapolis: University of Minnesota Press.

Gardner, D. 2002. "How cities license off-street hookers." *Ottawa Citizen*, 16 June. http://www.missingpeople.net/how_cities_'license'_off-street _hookers-june_16,_2002.htm

Gelder, K. 2007. *Subcultures: Cultural histories and social practice*. New York: Routledge.

Gifford, J. 2015. *Street poison: The biography of Iceberg Slim*. New York: Doubleday.

Gillies, K. 2013. "A wolf in sheep's clothing: Canadian anti-pimping law and how it hurts sex workers." In *Selling sex: Experience, advocacy and research on sex work in Canada*, edited by E. van der Meulen, E. Durisin, and V. Love, 269–78. Vancouver: UBC Press.

Gillies, K., and C. Bruckert. 2018. "Regulating sex workers' relationships: Partners and third Parties. In *Sex/work: Regulation, agency, and resistance*, edited by E. Durisin, E. van der Meulen, C. Bruckert. Vancouver: UBC Press.

Gleeson, K. 2004. " 'Having sunk as low as possible for a man to sink' – The pimp in law." *Australian Feminist Law Journal*, 21 (1): 101–20. https://doi.org/ 10.1080/13200968.2004.10854333

Goffman, E. 1956. *The presentation of self in everyday life*. Edinburgh: Social Sciences Research Centre, University of Edinburgh.

Goffman, E. 1963. *Stigma: Notes on the management of spoiled identity*. Englewood Cliffs, NJ: Prentice Hall.

Gonzales, J. 2010. "Booth rental: Is it right for you?" *Hairdresser Career Development Systems* (blog). http://hcds4you.com/booth-rental-is-it-right -for-you/

Government of New Zealand. 2004. *A guide to occupational health and safety in the New Zealand sex industry*. Wellington: Department of Labour, Occupational Health and Safety Service.

Government of New Zealand. 2008. *Report of the Prostitution Law Review Committee on the operation of the Prostitution Reform Act 2003*. Wellington: Ministry of Justice.

Government of Norway. 2004. *Purchasing sexual services in Sweden and the Netherlands: Legal regulation and experiences. An abbreviated English version*. A report by a working group on the legal regulation of the purchase of sexual services. Oslo: Ministry of Justice and Police.

Greenwald, H. 1958. *The call girl: A social and psychoanalytic study*. New York: Ballantine Books.

Hachey, I. 2004. "Danse érotique. Les Roumaines ont remplacé les Québécoises en Ontario." *La Presse* (Montreal), 23 December.

Hall, K. 2007. "Mansion Madam hits circuit to save house." *Windsor Star*, 19 January.http://www.pressreader.com/canada/windsor-star/20070119/281530811546367

Hall, S. 1979. "Culture, the media and the 'ideological effect.' " In *Mass communication and society*, edited by J. Curran, M. Gurevitch, and J. Woollacott, 315–47. London: E. Arnold and Open University Press.

Hall, S. 1997. "The work of representation." In *Representation, cultural representation and signifying practices*, edited by Stuart Hall, 15–74. London: Sage and Open University Press.

Ham, J. 2011. *What's the cost of a rumour? A guide to sorting out the myths and the facts about sporting events and trafficking.* Bangkok: Global Alliance Against Trafficking in Women.

Hanes, A. 2002a. "Prostitution sting stuns Quebec City, local luminaries alleged as clients." *National Post* (Toronto), 19 December.

Hanes, A. 2002b. "Parents unaware children working as prostitutes." *National Post* (Toronto), 21 December.

Hannem, S. 2012. "Theorizing stigma and the politics of resistance." In *Stigma revisited: Implications of the mark*, edited by S. Hannem, and C. Bruckert, 10–28. Ottawa: University of Ottawa Press.

Hannem, S., and C. Bruckert. 2012. "Concluding reflections: Academic activism and a call to action." In *Stigma revisited: Implications of the mark*, edited by S. Hannem an C. Bruckert, 176–82. Ottawa: University of Ottawa Press.

Hannem, S., and C. Bruckert. 2014. "Legal moralism, feminist rhetoric and the criminalization of consensual sex in Canada. In *Critical perspectives on women and the law in Canada*, edited by J. Kilty, 318–43. Vancouver: UBC Press.

Hannem, S., and C. Bruckert. 2016. " 'I'm not a pimp, but I play one on TV': The moral career and identity negotiations of third parties in the sex industry." *Deviant Behavior*, 38 (7): 824–36. http://www.tandfonline.com/doi/full/10.1080/01639625.2016.1197700

HIV/AIDS Legal Network. 2006. "Sex, work, rights: Reforming Canadian criminal laws on prostitution." Paper presented at the 7th Alberta Harm Reduction Conference, Lethbridge, AB.

Hochschild, A. R. 2003. *The managed heart: Commercialization of human feeling*, 2nd ed. Berkeley: University of California Press.

Hoigard, C., and L. Finstad. 1992. *Backstreets: Prostitution, money and love.* University Park: Pennsylvania University Press.

Holsopple, K. 1998. *Strip club testimony*. Minneapolis MN: Freedom and Justice Center for Prostitution Resources.

Holsopple, K. 1999. "Pimps, tricks, and feminists." *Women's Studies Quarterly*, 27 (1/2): 47–52.

Jackson, C. A. 2011. "Revealing contemporary constructions of femininity: Expression and sexuality in strip club legislation." *Sexualities*, 14 (3): 354–69. https://doi.org/10.1177/1363460711400964

Jackson, R. 2006. *Scripting the black masculine body: Identity, discourse, and racial politics in popular media.* Albany: State University of New York Press.

Jeffrey, L. A., and G. MacDonald. 2006. *Sex workers in the Maritimes talk back.* Vancouver: UBC Press.

Jeffrey, L. A., and B. Sullivan. 2009. "Canadian sex work policy for the 21st century: Enhancing rights and safety, lessons from Australia." *Canadian Political Science Review*, 3 (1): 57–76.

Jimenez, M. 2000a. "Running scared in new land: A young Hungarian woman planned to be a waitress, and maybe a singer, when she replied to an ad to come to Canada. Instead, her passport was taken and she was forced into sexual slavery. Two months later, she escaped." *National Post* (Toronto), 20 May.

Jimenez, M. 2000b. "Ottawa helpless to stop global sex traffic, thousands of women and children bought and sold." *National Post* (Toronto), 17 May.

Jiwani, Y. 2011. "Mediations of race and crime: Racializing crime, criminalizing race. In *Diversity, crime and justice in Canada*, edited by P. Barbara, 39–56. Toronto: Oxford University Press.

Johnson, G. J. 2015. "Governing sex work: An agonistic policy community and its relational dynamics." *Critical Policy Studies*, 9 (3): 259–77. https://doi.org/10.1080/19460171.2014.968602

Karandikar, S., and M. Prospero. 2010. "From client to pimp: Male violence against female sex workers." *Journal of Interpersonal Violence*, 25 (2): 257–73. https://doi.org/10.1177/0886260509334393

Kavemann, B., and H. Rabe. 2007. *The Act Regulating the Legal Situation of Prostitutes – implementation, impact, current developments: Findings of a study on the impact of the German Prostitution Act.* Berlin: Sozialwissenschaftliches Frauen Forschungs Institut.

Kilty, J. 2013. The mark of mental illness. In *Stigma revisited: Implications of the mark*, edited by S. Hannem and C. Bruckert, 176–82. Ottawa: University of Ottawa Press.

Klee, S. 2005. "The German Prostitution Act: Consequences for sex workers." In *Report of the European conference on sex work, human rights, labour and migration*, edited by A. Sorfleet, 53–57. Brussels: International Committee on the Rights of Sex Workers in Europe. http://www.walnet.org/csis/groups/icrse/brussels-2005/SWRights-German.pdf

Knight, D. 2010. "The (continuing) regulation of prostitution by local authorities." In *Taking the crime out of sex work: New Zealand sex workers' fight for decriminalization*, edited by G. Abel, L. Fitzgerald, C. Healy, and A. Taylor, 141–57. Bristol, UK: Polity Press. https://doi.org/10.1332/policypress/9781847423344.003.0009.

Kochman, T. 1981. *Black and white styles in conflict*. Chicago: University of Chicago Press.

Koskela, H. 2012. " 'You shouldn't wear that body': The problematic of surveillance and gender." In *Routledge handbook of surveillance studies*, edited by K. Ball, K. Haggerty, and D. Lyon, 49–56. New York: Routledge. https://doi.org/10.4324/9780203814949.ch1_2_a

Kovach, M. 2005. "Emerging from the margins: Indigenous methodologies." In *Research as resistance: Critical, indigenous and anti-oppressive approaches*, edited by L. Brown and S. Strega, 19–36. Toronto: Canadian Scholars' Press.

Krüsi, A., J. Chettiar, A. Ridgway, J. Abbott, S. Strathdee, and K. Shannon. 2012. "Negotiating safety and sexual risk reduction with clients in unsanctioned safer indoor sex work environments: A qualitative study." *American Journal of Public Health*, 102 (6): 1154–59. https://doi.org/10.2105/AJPH.2011.300638

Krüsi, A., K. Pacey, L. Bird. 2014. "Criminalisation of clients: Reproducing vulnerabilities for violence and poor health among street-based sex workers in Canada – a qualitative study." *BMJ Open*, 4 (6): 1–10.

Laing, M. 2012. "Regulating adult work in Canada: The role of criminal and municipal code. In *Policing sex*, edited by P. Johnson and D. Dalton, 166–84. New York: Routledge.

Lakeman, L., A. Lee, and S. Jay. 2004. "Resisting the promotion of prostitution in Canada: A view from the Vancouver Rape Relief and Women's Shelter. In *Not for sale: Feminists resisting prostitution and pornography*, edited by C. Stark and R. Whisnant, 210–55. Melbourne, AU: Spinifex Press.

Lavin, M. F. 2013. "Rule-making and rule-breaking: Strip club social control regarding alcohol and other drugs." *Deviant Behavior*, 34 (5): 361–83. https://doi.org/10.1080/01639625.2012.735611

Law, T. 2011. "Not a sob story: Transitioning out of sex work." MA thesis, University of Ottawa.

Law, T. 2012. "Cashing in on cachet? Ethnicity and gender in the strip club." *Canadian Journal of Women and the Law*, 24 (1): 135–53. https://doi.org/10.3138/cjwl.24.1.135

Law, T. 2016. "Managing the 'party': Third parties and the organization of labour in Ontario strip clubs." PhD diss., University of Ottawa.

Lazarus, L., K. Deering, R. Nabess, K. Gibson, M. Tyndall, and K. Shannon. 2012. "Occupational stigma as a primary barrier to health care for street-based sex workers in Canada." *Culture, Health & Sexuality*, 14 (2): 139–50. https://doi.org/10.1080/13691058.2011.628411

Leong, M. 2009. "Girl, 3, used as pawn to force mom into prostitution: Police." *National Post* (Toronto), 30 April.

Levy, J., and P. Jakobsson. 2013. "Abolitionist feminism as patriarchy control: Swedish understandings of prostitution and trafficking." *Dialectical Anthropology*, 37 (2): 333–40. https://doi.org/10.1007/s10624-013-9309-y

Lewis, J. 1999. "Controlling lap dancing: Law, morality and sex work." In *Sex for sale: Prostitution, pornography and the sex industry*, edited by R. Weitzer, 203–16. New York: Routledge.

Lewis, J. 2000. Controlling lap dancing: Law, morality and sex work. In *Sex for sale: Prostitution, pornography and the sex industry*, edited by R. Weitzer, 203–16. New York: Routledge.

Lewis, J. 2006. " 'I'll scratch your back if you'll scratch mine': The role of reciprocity, power and autonomy in the strip club." *Canadian Review of Sociology and Anthropology. La Revue Canadienne de Sociologie et d'Anthropologie*, 43 (3): 297–311. https://doi.org/10.1111/j.1755-618X.2006.tb02226.x

Lewis, J., and E. Maticka-Tyndale. 2000. "Licensing sex work: Public policy and women's lives." *Canadian Public Policy*, 26 (4): 437–49. https://doi.org/10.2307/3552610

Lewis, J., E. Maticka-Tyndale, F. Shaver, and H. Schramm. 2005. "Managing risk and safety on the job: The experiences of Canadian sex workers." *Journal of Psychology & Human Sexuality*, 17 (1–2): 147–67. https://doi.org/10.1300/J056v17n01_09

Lewis, J., and F. Shaver. 2006. *Safety, security and the well-being of sex workers: A report to the House of Commons Subcommittee on Solicitation Laws*. Windsor, ON: Sex Trade Advocacy and Research.

Lewis, P., A. Thornhill, and M. Saunders. 2003. *Employee relations: Understanding the employment relationship*. Essex, UK: Pearson Education.

Lilleston, P., J. Reuben, and S. Sherman. 2012. " 'This is our sanctuary': Perceptions of safety among exotic dancers in Baltimore, Maryland." *Health & Place*, 18 (3): 561–67. https://doi.org/10.1016/j.healthplace.2012.01.009

Lofaro, J. 2014. "New prostitution laws could be 'disincentive' for johns to report underage sex workers: Professor." *Metro* (Ottawa), 14 November.

Louis, M. V. 1991. "Prostitution, proxénétisme, traite des êtres humains." *Prostitution et droits de la personne. Cette violence dont nous ne voulons plus*, numéro spécial (11/12): 3–10.

Louis, M. V. 2006. "Cette violence dont nous ne voulons plus. À propos des nouvelles approches en matière de prostitution et de proxénétisme." *Chronique féministe*, Prostitution et feminism (51): 15–20.

Love, V. 2013. "Champagne, strawberries, and truck-stop motels: On subjectivity and sex work." In *Selling sex: Experience, advocacy, and research on sex work in Canada*, edited by E. van der Meulen, E. Durisin, and V. Love, 103–13. Vancouver: UBC Press.

Lowman, J. 1986. "Street prostitution in Vancouver: Notes on the genesis of a social problem." *Canadian Journal of Criminology*, 28 (1): 1–16.

Lowman, J. 2000. "Violence and the outlaw status of (street) prostitution in Canada." *Violence against Women*, 6 (9): 987–1011. https://doi.org/10.1177/10778010022182245

Lowman, J. 2005. "Submission to the Subcommittee on Solicitation Laws." http://mypage.uniserve.ca/~lowman/

MacDonald, G. 2004. " 'I wanted … to capture the real horror of it.' " *Globe and Mail* (Toronto), 9 October.

Machen, H. 1996. "Women's work: Attitudes, regulation, and lack of power within the sex industry." *Hastings Women's Law Journal*, 7 (1): 177–200.

MacKay, P. 2014. "Presentation to the Standing Committee on Justice and Human Rights." Evidence of Proceedings, 41st Parl., 2nd sess., meetings no. 32.

Mancini, J. G. (1962) 1972. *Prostitution et proxénétisme*. Paris: Presses universitaires de France.

Mandel, C. 2007. "N.S. teens lured to city, life of crime." *National Post* (Toronto), 26 October.

Maticka-Tyndale, E. 2004. *Exotic dancing in Ontario: Health and safety*. Windsor, ON: Sex Trade Advocacy and Research.

Maticka-Tyndale, E., J. Lewis, J. P. Clark, J. Zubick, and S. Young. 1999. "Social and cultural vulnerability to sexually transmitted infection: The work of exotic dancers." *Canadian Journal of Public Health*, 90 (1): 19–22.

Maticka-Tyndale, E., J. Lewis, J. P. Clark, J. Zubick, and S. Young. 2000. "Exotic dancing and health." *Women & Health*, 31 (1): 87–108. https://doi.org/10.1300/J013v31n01_06

May, T., A. Harocopos, and M. Hough. 2000. *For love or money: Pimps and the management of sex work*. London: Home Office, Police Research Series, Paper 134.

McKeganey, N., and M. Barnard. 1996. *Sex work on the streets: Prostitutes and their clients*. Philadelphia, PA: Open University Press.

Mensah, M. N. 2006. "Débat féministe sur la prostitution au Québec: Points de vue des travailleuses du sexe." *Canadian Review of Sociology and Anthropology. La Revue Canadienne de Sociologie et d'Anthropologie*, 43 (3): 345–61. https://doi.org/10.1111/j.1755-618X.2006.tb02229.x

Millar, H., and T. O'Doherty. 2015. *The Palermo Protocol & Canada: The evolution and human rights impacts of anti-trafficking laws in Canada (2002–2015).* Vancouver: SWAN Vancouver Society.

Miller, J. 1995. "Gender and power on the streets: Street prostitution in the era of crack cocaine." *Journal of Contemporary Ethnography*, 23 (4): 427–52. https://doi.org/10.1177/089124195023004002

Miller, M. 2014. "Presentation to the Standing Committee on Justice and Human Rights." Evidence of Proceedings, 41st Parl., 2nd sess., meetings no. 39.

Milner, C., and R. Milner. 1972. *Black players: The secret world of black pimps.* New York: Little Brown and Co.

Mitchel, B. 2007. "Man charged in brutal sex assault gets bail." *Toronto Star*, 2 August.

MLS [Municipal Licensing and Standards]. 2012a. *Review of adult entertainment parlour regulations.* Toronto: City of Toronto.

MLS [Municipal Licensing and Standards]. 2012b. *Review of adult entertainment regulations: Amendments to Toronto Municipal Code chapter 545.* Toronto: City of Toronto.

Morris, M., and B. Bunjun. 2007. *Using intersectional feminist frameworks in research: A resource for embracing the complexities of women's lives.* Ottawa: Canadian Research Institute for the Advancement of Women.

Mossman, E. 2010. "Brothel operators' and support agencies' experiences of decriminalization." In *Taking the crime out of sex work: New Zealand sex workers' fight for decriminalization*, edited by G. Abel, L. Fitzgerald, C. Healy, and A. Taylor, 119–40. Portland, OR: Policy Press.

Murphy, A. G. 2003. "The dialectical gaze." *Journal of Contemporary Ethnography*, 32 (3): 305–35. https://doi.org/10.1177/0891241603032003003

New South Wales. 2006. *Sex services premises: Planning guideline.* Sydney: Department of Planning. Sex Services Premises Planning Advisory Panel.

Norton-Hawk, M. 2004. "A comparison of pimp- and non-pimp-controlled women." *Violence against Women*, 10 (2): 189–94. https://doi.org/10.1177/1077801203260949

O'Connell, D. J. 1998. *Prostitution, power and freedom.* Ann Arbor: University of Michigan Press.

O'Doherty, T. 2011. "Criminalization and off-street sex work in Canada." *Canadian Journal of Criminology and Criminal Justice*, 53 (2): 217–45. https://doi.org/10.3138/cjccj.53.2.217

Overs, C., and B. Loff. 2013. "Towards a legal framework that promotes and protects sex workers' health and human rights." *Health and Human Rights*, 15 (1): 186–96.

Parent, C., and C. Bruckert. 2005. "Répondre aux besoins des travailleuses du sexe de rue: Un objectif qui passe par la décriminalisation de leurs activités de travail." *Reflets (Sudbury)*, 11 (1): 112–45. https://doi.org/10.7202/013061ar

Parent, C., and C. Bruckert. 2013. "The current debate on sex work." In *Sex work: Rethinking the job, respecting the workers*, edited by C. Parent, C. Bruckert, P. Corriveau, N. Mensah, L. Toupin, 9–30. Vancouver: UBC Press.

Parliamentary Subcommittee on Solicitation Laws (SSLR). 2006. *The challenge of change: A study of Canada's criminal prostitution laws*. Ottawa: Standing Committee on Justice and Human Rights.

Patrick, K. 2007. "Canadian-born stripper hit with racketeering in U.S." *National Post* (Toronto), 12 January.

Pheterson, G. 1996. *The prostitution prism*. Amsterdam: Amsterdam University Press.

Pires, A. 1997. *De quelques enjeux épistémologiques d'une méthodologie générale pour les sciences sociales*. Montréal: Centre international de criminologie comparée, Université de Montréal.

Pitts, A. 2015. *Remembering Bedford: The impacts of criminalization on street-based sex workers*. MA thesis, York University.

PIVOT Legal Society. 2006. *Beyond decriminalization: Sex work, human rights and a new framework for law reform*. Vancouver: PIVOT Legal Society.

Poulin, R. 2003. "Prostitution, crime organisé et marchandisation." *Revue Tiers Monde*, 44 (176): 736–69. https://doi.org/10.3406/tiers.2003.5425

Poulin, R. 2004. *La mondialisation des industries du sexe. Prostitution, pornographie, traite des femmes et des enfants*. Ottawa: L'Interligne.

POWER. 2014. "Ottawa-area sex workers targets of intrusive police visits." Press release, 26 January. http://www.powerottawa.ca/POWER%20 press%20release%20-%20January%202014%20OPS%20visits%20FINAL.pdf

Price, K. 2008. " 'Keeping the dancers in check': The gendered organization of stripping work at the Lion's Den." *Gender & Society*, 22 (3): 367–89. https://doi.org/10.1177/0891243208316518

Price-Glynn, K. 2010. *Strip club: Gender, power and sex work*. New York: New York University Press.

Prior, J., and P. Crofts. 2015. "Is your house a brothel? Prostitution policy, provision of sex services from home, and the maintenance of respectable domesticity." *Social Policy and Society*, 14 (01): 125–34. https://doi.org/10.1017/S1474746414000335

Quinn, E. 2000. " 'Who's the Mack?': The performativity and politics of the pimp figure in gangsta rap." *Journal of American Studies*, 34 (1): 115–36. https://doi.org/10.1017/S0021875899006295

Raphael, J., and B. Myers-Powell. 2009. *Interviews with five ex-pimps in Chicago*. Chicago: De Paul University College of Law.

Raphael, J., and B. Myers-Powell. 2010. *From victims to victimizers: Interviews with 25 ex-pimps in Chicago*. Chicago: Schiller DuCanto and Fleck Family Law Center of DePaul University College of Law.

Raphael, J., J. A. Reichert, and M. Powers. 2010. "Pimp control and violence: Domestic sex trafficking of Chicago women and girls." *Women & Criminal Justice*, 20 (1–2): 89–104. https://doi.org/10.1080/08974451003641065

Raphael, J., and D. L. Shapiro. 2004. "Violence in indoor and outdoor prostitution venues." *Violence Against Women*, 10 (2): 126–39. https://doi.org/10.1177/1077801203260529

Ratansi, Y. 2007. *Turning outrage into action to address trafficking for the purpose of sexual exploitation in Canada: Report of the Standing Committee on the Status of Women*. Ottawa: Communications Canada.

Ray, R. 2002. " 'A Crook and a dangerous man.' " *Globe and Mail* (Toronto), 25 May.

Reed, S. 1997. "All stripped off." In *Whores and other feminists*, edited by J. Nagel, 179–88. New York: Routledge

Reinharz, S. 1993. "Neglected voices and excessive demands in feminist research." *Qualitative Sociology*, 16 (1): 69–76. https://doi.org/10.1007/BF00990074

Renni, S. 2012. "Ottawa police seek girl, 17, in teen-pimp case, urge parents to monitor social media." Canadian Press, 12 June.

Rivers-Moore, M. 2016. *Gringo gulch: Sex, tourism and social mobility in Costa Rica*. Chicago: University of Chicago Press.

Roots, K. 2013. "Trafficking or pimping? An analysis of Canada's human trafficking legislation and its implications." *Canadian Journal of Law and Society*, 28 (1): 21–41. https://doi.org/10.1017/cls.2012.4

Ross, B. 2006. " 'Troublemakers' in tassels and g-strings: Striptease dancers and the union question in Vancouver, 1965–1980." *CRSA/RCSA*, 43 (3): 329–44.

Ross, B. 2009. *Burlesque west: Showgirls, sex, and sin in postwar Vancouver*. Toronto: University of Toronto Press.

Sanders, T. 2001. "Female street sex workers, sexual violence, and protection strategies." *Journal of Sexual Aggression*, 7 (1): 5–18. https://doi.org/10.1080/13552600108413318

Sanders, T. 2005. "Blinded by morality? Prostitution policy in the UK." *Capital and Class*, 29 (9): 9–15.

Sanghera, J. 2005. "Unpacking the trafficking discourse." In *Trafficking and prostitution reconsidered: New perspectives on migration, sex work, and human rights*, edited by K. Kempadoo, J. Sanghera, and B. Pattanaik, 3–24. New York: Routledge.

Schmitt, K. 2013. *Pimping: A symbolic manifestation of racism and street culture. Representing Subcultures & Social Movements* (blog). https://repsub13 .wordpress.com/projects/pimping/.

Séguin, R. 2002. "Web site lured girls, officials say." *Globe and Mail* (Toronto), 20 December.

Séguin, R. 2003. "Prostitution ring finished, Quebec City police say." *Globe and Mail* (Toronto), 16 May.

Selala, K. J. 2011. "The enforceability of illegal employment contracts according to the Labour Appeal Court: Comments on Kylie vs CCMA 2010 4 SA 383 (LAC)." *PER/PELJ*, 14 (2): 207–26.

Seymour, A. 2015. "Sending teen pimp to adult prison the right call, victim's mother says" *Ottawa Citizen*, 14 January.

Shaver, F. 1993. "Prostitution: A female crime." In *In conflict with the law: Women and the Canadian justice system*, edited by E. Adelberg and C. Currie, 153–73. Vancouver: Press Gang Publishers.

Shaver, F. 1996. "The regulation of prostitution: Setting the morality trap." In *Social control in Canada*, edited by B. Schissel and L. Mahood, 204–26. Oxford: Oxford University Press.

Shaver, F. 2005. "Sex work research: Methodological and ethical challenges." *Journal of Interpersonal Violence*, 20 (3): 296–319. https://doi.org/10.1177/ 0886260504274340

Shaver, F., J. Lewis, and E. Maticka-Tyndale. 2011. "Rising to the challenge: Addressing the concerns of people working in the sex industry. *Canadian Review of Sociology*, 48 (1): 47–65. https://doi.org/10.1111/j.1755 -618X.2011.01249.x

Silbert, M. H., and A. M. Pines. 1981. "Occupation hazards of street prostitutes." *Criminal Justice and Behavior*, 8 (4): 395–99. https://doi.org/ 10.1177/009385488100800401

Sirois, A. 2003. "Le trafic des êtres humains. DE mauvaises notes pour le Canada." *La Presse* (Montreal), 10 December.

Slim, I. 1967. *Pimp: The story of my life*. Edinburgh, UK: Payback Press.

Smith, S. 2003. "The control of prostitution: An update." NSW Parliamentary Library Research Service, Briefing Paper No 14/03.

Smith-Tague, K. 2014. "Presentation to the Standing Committee on Justice and Human Rights." Evidence of Proceedings, 41st Parl., 2nd sess., meetings no. 41.

Solanna, A., J. Xi Jia, L. Vivian, J. Chattier, A. Krüsi, S. Allan, L. Maher, and K. Shannon. 2015. "Violence prevention and municipal licensing of indoor sex work venues in the Greater Vancouver Area: Narratives of migrant sex workers, managers and business owners." *Culture, Health & Sexuality: An*

International Journal for Research, Intervention and Care, 17 (7): 825–41. http://dx.doi.org/10.1080/13691058.2015.1008046

Spidel, A., C. Greaves, B. S. Cooper, H. Hervé, R. D. Hare, J. C. Yuille. 2006. "The psychopath as pimp." *The Canadian Journal of Police & Security Services*, 4 (4): 193–99.

Staiger, A. 2005. " 'Hoes can be hoed out, players can be played out, but pimp is for life': The pimp phenomenon as strategy of identity formation. *Symbolic Interaction*, 28 (3): 407–28. https://doi.org/10.1525/si.2005.28.3.407

Stenvoll, D. 2002. "From Russia with love? Newspaper coverage of cross-border prostitution in northern Norway, 1990–2001." *European Journal of Women's Studies*, 9 (2): 143–62. https://doi.org/10.1177/1350682002009002807

Sullivan, B. 2010. "When (some) prostitution is legal: The impact of law reform on sex work in Australia." *Journal of Law and Society*, 37 (1): 85–104. https://doi.org/10.1111/j.1467-6478.2010.00496.x

Toupin, L. 2013. "Clandestine migrations by women and the risk of trafficking." In *Sex work: Rethinking the job, respecting the workers*, edited by C. Parent, C. Bruckert, P. Corriveau, N. Mensah, and L. Toupin, 111–32. Vancouver: UBC Press.

Trihn, J. 2012. "#dangerousliaisons: Inside the shocking online worlds of three teen girls charged with pimping out their friends." *Ottawa Magazine*. 27 September.

Truong, T. (2014). "Presentation to the Standing Committee on Justice and Human Rights." Evidence of Proceedings, 41st Parl., 2nd sess., meetings no. 38.

van der Meulen, E. 2010. "Illegal lives, loves, and work: How the criminalization of procuring affects sex workers in Canada." *Wagadu: A Journal of Transnational Women's and Gender Studies*, 8: 217–40.

van der Meulen, E. 2011. "Sex work and Canadian policy: Recommendations for labor legitimacy and social change." *Sexuality Research & Social Policy*, 8 (4): 348–58. https://doi.org/10.1007/s13178-011-0069-7

van der Meulen, E., and E. Durisin. 2008. "Why decriminalize? How Canada's municipal and federal regulations increase sex workers' vulnerability." *Canadian Journal of Women and the Law*, 20 (2): 289–311.

van der Meulen, E., E. Durisin, and V. Love. 2013. *Selling sex: Experience, advocacy, and research on sex work in Canada*. Vancouver: UBC Press.

van der Meulen, E., and M. Valverde. 2013. "Beyond the Criminal Code: Municipal licensing and zoning bylaws." In *Selling sex: Experience, advocacy, and research on sex work in Canada*, edited by E. van der Meulen, E. Durisin, and V. Love, 314–22. Vancouver: UBC Press.

Vosko, L. 2000. *Temporary work: The gendered rise of a precarious employment relationship*. Toronto: University of Toronto Press. https://doi.org/10.3138/9781442680432.

Vosko, L., M. MacDonald, and I. Campbell, eds. 2009. *Gender and the contours of precarious employment*. New York: Routledge.

Vosko, L., E. Tucker, and P. Mark. 2011. *New approaches to enforcement and compliance with labour regulatory standards: The case of Ontario, Canada comparative research in law and political economy network*. Toronto: York University Osgoode Hall Law School.

Vosko, L., N. Zukewich, and C. Cranford. 2003. "Precarious jobs: A new typology of employment." *Perspectives in Labour and Income*, 4 (10). http://www.statcan.gc.ca/pub/75-001-x/01003/6642-eng.html

Wagenaar, H. 2006. Democracy and prostitution: Deliberating the legalization of brothels in the Netherlands. *Administration & Society*, 38 (2): 198–235. https://doi.org/10.1177/0095399705285991

Wagenaar, H., and S. Altink. 2012. "Prostitution as morality politics or why it is exceedingly difficult to design and sustain effective prostitution policy." *Sexuality Research & Social Policy*, 9 (3): 279–92. https://doi.org/10.1007/s13178-012-0095-0

Wagenaar, H., S. Altink, and H. Amesberger. 2013. *Final report of the International Comparative Study of Prostitution Policy: Austria and the Netherlands*. Den Haag, NL: Platform 31.

Weitzer, R. 2005. "Flawed theory and method in studies of prostitution." *Violence against Women*, 11 (7): 934–49. https://doi.org/10.1177/1077801205276986

White, M., and K. Meaney. 2007. "Teenage girl 'sold' to pimp for cash and coke: Note; likely working in Montreal." *National Post* (Toronto), 22 September.

Willmott, H. 1997. "Rethinking management and managerial work: Capitalism, control and subjectivity." *Human Relations*, 50 (11): 1329–59. https://doi.org/10.1177/001872679705001101

Winick, C., and P. Kinsie. 1971. *The lively commerce: Prostitution in the United States*. Chicago: Quadrangle Books.

Wojcik, D. 2010. "Pimp walk." In *Encyclopedia of African American Popular Culture*, vol. 1, edited by Jessie Carney Smith, 1089–91). Westport, CT: Greenwood.

Young, A. P. 2000. " 'I'm just me': A study of managerial resistance." *Journal of Organizational Change Management*, 13 (4): 375–88. https://doi.org/10.1108/09534810010339068

YWCA. 2008. *Beauty at any cost*. Washington: YWCA USA.

Cases Cited

Bedford v. Canada, 2010 ONSC 4264.
Canada (Attorney General) v. Bedford, 2012 ONCA 186.
City of Toronto v. Zanzibar Tavern Inc., 2007 ONCJ 401.
R. v. Pelletier, 2016 ONCJ 628.

Legislation Cited

Canadian Charter of Rights and Freedoms, Part I of the Constitution Act, 1982, being Schedule B to the Canada Act 1982 (UK), 1982, c 11.
City of Ottawa. 2004. By-law No. 2002–189, *Adult Entertainment Parlours – Schedule 11.*
City of Toronto. 2012. By-law No. 243–2013, *To amend City of Toronto Municipal Code Chapter 545, licensing, respecting adult entertainment parlours.*
Criminal Code, RSC 1985, c C-46 s 745.
Ontario Municipal Act, 2001.
Prostitution Reform Act, New Zealand, 2003.
Protection of Communities and Exploited Persons Act [Bill C-36: An Act to Amend the Criminal Code in Response to the Supreme Court of Canada Decision in Attorney General of Canada v Bedford and to Make Consequential Amendments to Other Acts], 2014, 2nd session, 41st Parliament.
Toronto Municipal Code, c545 art 32, 2010.

Contributors

Chris Bruckert is a professor in the department of criminology at the University of Ottawa. Over the past twenty years she has devoted much of her energy to examining diverse sectors of the sex industry and has undertaken qualitative research into street-based sex work, erotic dance, incall and outcall sex work, clients, male sex workers, and third parties in the sex industry. Chris Bruckert has authored over forty peer-reviewed publications on the sex industry, is the author of *Taking It Off, Putting It On: Women in the Strip Trade*, and co-editor of *Stigma Revisited* and *Mais oui c'est un travail* (available in English as *Sex Work: Rethinking the Job, Respecting the Workers*).

Patrice Corriveau is a sociologist and a full professor in the department of criminology at the University of Ottawa. He is the author of several books and has worked as a senior policy analyst at the Canadian Department of Justice.

Tuulia Law is a sessional assistant professor at York University. She completed her PhD in criminology at the University of Ottawa in 2016. Her doctoral research, an offshoot of the Management Project, used the data from the erotic dance sector alongside additional interviews she collected later. Through the Management Project and her doctoral dissertation she became interested in performances and manipulations of masculinity, which she looks forward to exploring in greater depth in regard to the sex industry, professional sports, and popular culture. She has recently been published in the *Canadian Journal of Law and Society*, and has contributed chapters to *Expanding the Gaze: Gender and the Politics of Surveillance* (University of Toronto Press, 2016) and *Selling Sex:*

Experience, Advocacy, and Research on Sex Work in Canada (UBC Press, 2013).

Leslie Ann Jeffrey is a professor of comparative politics and international relations at the University of New Brunswick, Saint John. She is author of a number of articles on sex work, trafficking, and policy. She is also the co-author of *Sex Workers in the Maritimes Talk Back* (UBC Press, 2006) and author of *Sex and Borders: Gender, National Identity and Prostitution Policy in Thailand* (UBC Press, 2002).

Maria Nengeh Mensah is a professor of social work and feminist studies at Université du Québec à Montréal, a community advocate, and the mother of two boys. She has been involved in the fight against HIV/ AIDS in Canada since 1989 and in the international movement for sex workers' rights since 1999. She has published extensively on issues of media discourse and messaging, the challenges of social stigmatization, and third-wave feminism. She co-authored the books *Sex Work: Rethinking the Job, Respecting the Workers* (UBC Press, 2013) and *Luttes XXX: Inspirations du mouvement des travailleuses du sexe* (Remue-ménage, 2011). Over the last decade, Mensah has also developed training materials and awareness tools for people who provide services to the public (community, health, and social services, police, and media).

Colette Parent (PhD in criminology) is a retired professor in the department of criminology at the University of Ottawa. She writes in the areas of women and criminal justice, in particular on the criminalization of women, sex work, violence against women as partners, and on feminism's contribution to criminology. She has completed several empirical researches on different types of sex work (in the streets, massage parlours, and erotic establishments, in erotic bars, and by women, men, and trans). She has devoted herself to researching the theoretical debates on "prostitution" and on developing our understanding of sex work as a form of work in the service sector. In her publications Parent has underlined the need to use as a point of departure the sex workers' world and standpoint to observe sex work as a form of work. Through her analysis of the contemporary debate on sex work, she continues to shed light on myths and prejudice faced by sex workers.

www.ingramcontent.com/pod-product-compliance
Lightning Source LLC
Chambersburg PA
CBHW030248030426
42336CB00009B/301